D1329701

Multicultural Literature in the Content Areas

Multicultural Literature in the Content Areas

Transforming K–12 Classrooms Into Engaging, Inviting, and Socially Conscious Spaces

Lakia M. Scott
Barbara Purdum-Cassidy

ROWMAN & LITTLEFIELD
Lanham • Boulder • New York • London

Published by Rowman & Littlefield
An imprint of The Rowman & Littlefield Publishing Group, Inc.
4501 Forbes Boulevard, Suite 200, Lanham, Maryland 20706
www.rowman.com

6 Tinworth Street, London SE11 5AL, United Kingdom

British Library Cataloguing in Publication Information Available

Library of Congress Cataloging-in-Publication Data

Names: Scott, Lakia, editor. | Purdum-Cassidy, Barbara, editor.
Title: Multicultural literature in the content areas : transforming K–12
    classrooms into engaging, inviting, and socially conscious spaces /
    edited by Lakia M. Scott, Barbara Purdum-Cassidy.
Description: Lanham, Maryland : Rowman & Littlefield Publishing Group,
    2020. | Includes bibliographical references and index. | Summary: "This
    text seeks to remedy the single-story paradigm that is often utilized in
    the literary canon by providing multicultural literature and
    supplementary resources that can be used across disciplines and grade
    levels. A more in-depth understanding of using inquiry-based approaches
    alongside multicultural literature in the classroom is provided"—
    Provided by publisher.
Identifiers: LCCN 2019046547 (print) | LCCN 2019046548 (ebook) | ISBN
    9781475853520 (cloth) | ISBN 9781475853537 (paperback) | ISBN
    9781475853544 (epub)
Subjects: LCSH: Culturally relevant pedagogy. | Multiculturalism in literature.
Classification: LCC LC1099.515.C85 M85 2020 (print) | LCC LC1099.515.C85
    (ebook) | DDC 370.117—dc23
LC record available at https://lccn.loc.gov/2019046547
LC ebook record available at https://lccn.loc.gov/2019046548

∞™ The paper used in this publication meets the minimum requirements of American National Standard for Information Sciences—Permanence of Paper for Printed Library Materials, ANSI/NISO Z39.48-1992.

Contents

Section One: Using Multicultural Literature in English Language Arts, Reading, and Social Studies

Section Two: Using Multicultural Literature for Science and Mathematics

Acknowledgments

I feel it most important to first acknowledge my ancestors, Hattie, John Elliot (J. E.), and Paul (Pete), among others in my family lineage, who persisted throughout their lifetime in order for future generations to have access to an education where one can feel empowered, inspired, and most of all liberated. I am reminded of your presence when I feel the gentle, subtle nudge to endure during times of challenge and in the light, airy moments of triumph.

Second, I would like to acknowledge my immediate and extended family members who have labored to continue community building despite circumstance and sacrifice. Specifically, my husband and I are blessed to have welcomed our second son, Levyn, into this world during a time when diversity and inclusion are boldly represented in children's literature to serve not only as a symbol of culture, community, and voice, but also as a beacon of hope for unity among all people despite difference.

Finally, I must acknowledge the Baylor School of Education, and members of the Department of Curriculum and Instruction, for continuing to support my research and academic vision. And to Barbara, my dear friend, I am most thankful for you—you are such a light, and I am grateful for our friendship that has spurred from our various projects together.

—Lakia M. Scott

First and foremost, I am so grateful to our collaborating authors for their contributions to this book. I also wish to acknowledge our reviewers, who provided outstanding feedback on each chapter that greatly improved our final product.

I feel fortunate to have worked with an extraordinary Rowman & Littlefield team, particularly our editor, Sarah Jubar. Sarah, thank you for supporting this project every step of the way. Your feedback, insightful thinking, and constant encouragement are greatly appreciated.

Lakia, I am thankful for your continuing friendship. I have been fortunate to work with you on many projects, and it is an honor to teach, work, and learn alongside you.

I'd like to thank my husband, Dan. Your sense of humor and wisdom inspire me to be my best. You continually tell me how proud you are of me. That is all the affirmation I will ever need.

—Barbara Purdum-Cassidy

Introduction

Lakia M. Scott

The necessity for multicultural education practices in public schools has never been more vital as today's classrooms represent more racially and culturally diverse students than ever before. In turn, culturally responsive and affirming teaching practices should mirror the academic, social, and cultural needs of an ever-increasing population of diverse students. Multicultural education is a theory and practice that provides opportunity for discussion and dialogue that centers on issues of race, class, gender, disability, sexuality, and religion in society (Banks, 1993).

As Banks (1993) notes, a major goal in multicultural education is to reform practices in schools so students from diverse social and cultural backgrounds experience educational equality. Conceptualized through a five-dimensional framework of content integration, knowledge construction, prejudice reduction, equity pedagogy, and empowering school culture and social structure, the aims of multicultural education center on social justice, equity, and inclusion. Multicultural education practices provide mutually beneficial dialogue for when spaces represent difference, and the pedagogical practices increase learning outcomes for all students who are participatory in the content (Osorio, 2018).

Ladson-Billings (1994) and Gay (2000) advocate for culturally relevant and responsive teaching in light of today's subpar educational conditions. In the midst of standardized assessments, high-stakes testing, and streamlined curriculum standards, it is important to modify pedagogy to adapt to student needs and those of the communities in which they reside. In literacy, this role is especially important (Gay, 2000; Ladson-Billings, 1994).

In order for students to be successful learners, the connection between textbooks, stories, and curricula must be multicultural, reflexive, and critical

(Freire, 2000; Gay, 2000; Ladson-Billings, 1994; Nieto, 1992). By exposing students to critical information, students can make vital connections between education and social problems. In the most organic sense, education becomes a tool for critical inquiry and questioning.

One example of utilizing multicultural literature in curriculum is the Children's Defense Fund (CDF) Freedom School national program model. Established in the 1990s as a six-week summer literacy program, CDF Freedom Schools provides academic enrichment to working and middle-class K–12 students through culturally relevant and developmentally appropriate literature. Using the varied readings—some of which are biographical sketches of historical change agents—participants are empowered to make a difference in themselves, their communities, and the world through reading.

In addition, students partake in a National Day of Social Action where they conduct research on a pertinent social issue, such as child hunger, gun violence, or neighborhood safety, and then develop an action plan to become civically engaged. Westheimer and Kahn (2004) would suggest these actions to be participatory and social justice oriented, both of which positively impact change in our society.

In this way, the utilization of multicultural literature becomes a vehicle for promoting social justice, equity, and inclusion in academic spaces. There are many benefits to having this type of resource in classrooms: (1) Students visually see more representations of themselves presented in the literature and, as a result, become more empowered in the classroom; (2) students become more engaged and motivated toward reading, thereby increasing student academic outcomes; and (3) the classroom disrupts mainstream ideologies and narratives presented in traditional literary canons. Other studies point to multicultural literature as a means to affirm students' social and cultural identities and to increase their understanding of the world around them (Harper & Brand, 2012).

Additional studies have investigated how the use of culturally relevant texts influences teacher effectiveness in the classroom. Leonard, Moore, and Brooks (2013) conducted a study that applied multicultural texts as a context for teaching mathematics in a teacher education course. Findings revealed that the majority of the teacher-candidate-created lessons had increased elements of cultural competence and critical consciousness—as developed from the integration of multicultural children's literature.

In this way, multicultural literature has the power to transform traditional classrooms into spaces that are engaging, inviting, critically reflective, and socially conscious in order to enact societal change. As such, this book provides ten chapters that explore various multicultural texts for K–12 classrooms. The book is organized into two sections: *Using Multicultural*

Literature in English Language Arts, Reading, and Social Studies and *Using Multicultural Literature in Science and Mathematics.*

In the first section, Kelly Johnston begins by emphasizing critical consciousness in literacy instruction to consider perspectives and lived experiences among students. Most importantly, teachers are encouraged to be reflexive and cognizant of cultural competency as articulated through the lesson. Second, Elena Venegas targets reading comprehension for students by utilizing the pedagogical strategy developed by Raphael (1986), Question-Answer Relationships. By understanding these relationships, students can answer both explicit and implicit questions about what they are reading.

Next, Janet Keeler uses food themes to increase community among students as a means to increase cultural awareness and foster inclusivity when faced with difficult social and cultural topics. Kevin Magill also explores culture circles and critical inquiry as a technique for teaching social studies within a social justice framework. Finally, Sarah Straub places emphasis on culturally responsive teaching practices by engaging students to make connections to characters' experiences and emotions.

In the second section, chapters focus on the utilization of multicultural literature while teaching science and mathematics. In Chapter 6, Yasmin Laird uses inquiry circles and project-based learning in order to present activities to stimulate thinking about historical figures in science. Example lessons foster students' ability to make connections to the experiments and become innovators by also thinking about their own possible inventions and experiments. Christine Picot, in Chapter 7, examines the significance of using storytelling and problem-solving skills in mathematics content.

Next, Amy Corp reveals an emphasis on collaborative grouping and mathematical thinking in order to help students to better understand and examine the character's experiences during the Jim Crow era. Following, Jamie Wong uses problem solving and project-based learning in order to allow the student to become both researcher and activist. Particularly moving in this chapter is the emphasis for students to present and examine historical and contemporary statistical data in connection to the book's contents and aims on social justice. In the final chapter, Amy Corp utilizes prior knowledge, problem solving, and connection building to mathematical content to bridge students' comprehension.

REFERENCES

Banks, J. A. (1993). Multicultural education: Historical development, dimensions, and practice. *Review of Research in Education, 19*(1), 3–49.

Children's Defense Fund. (2015). CDF Freedom Schools program. Retrieved on May 19, 2017, from www.childrensdefense.org/programs/freedomschools

Ching, S. D. (2005). Multicultural children's literature as an instrument of power. *Language Arts, 83*(2), 128–136.

Freire, P. (2000). *Pedagogy of freedom: Ethics, democracy, and civic courage.* Lanham, MD: Rowman & Littlefield Publishers.

Gay, G. (2000). *Culturally responsive teaching: Theory, research, and practice.* New York: Teachers College Press.

Harper, L. J., & Brand, S. T. (2010, June). More alike than different: Promoting respect through multicultural books and literacy strategies. *Childhood Education, 86*(4), 224–233.

Ladson-Billings, G. (1994). What we can learn from multicultural education research. *Educational leadership, 51*(8), 22–26.

Leonard, J., Moore, C. M., & Brooks, W. (2013). Multicultural children's literature as a context for teaching mathematics for cultural relevance in urban schools. *Urban Review, 46*, 325–348.

Nieto, S. (1992). *Affirming diversity: The sociopolitical context of multicultural education.* White Plains, NY: Longman.

Osorio, S. L. (2018). Multicultural literature as a classroom tool. *Multicultural Perspectives, 20*(1), 47–52.

Raphael, T. E. (1986). Teaching question-answer relationships, revisited. *The Reading Teacher, 39*(6), 516–522.

Sims-Bishop, R. (1997). Selecting literature for a multicultural curriculum. In V. J. Harris (Ed.), *Using multiethnic literature in the K–8 classroom* (pp. 1–20). Norwood, MA: Christopher-Gordon.

Souto-Manning, M. (2009). Negotiating culturally responsive pedagogy through multicultural children's literature: Towards critical democratic literacy practices in a first-grade classroom. *Journal of Early Childhood Literacy, 9*(1), 50–74.

Taylor, D. B., Medina, A. L., & Lara-Cinisomo, S. (2010). *Freedom School partners Children's Defense Fund Freedom Schools Program evaluation report.* Center for Adolescent Literacies at UNC Charlotte.

Westheimer, J., & Kahn, J. (2004). What kind of citizen? The politics of educating for democracy. *American Education Research Journal, 41*(2), 237–269.

Section One

USING MULTICULTURAL
LITERATURE FOR ENGLISH LANGUAGE
ARTS, READING, AND SOCIAL STUDIES

1

The Day You Begin

Using Children's Lived Experiences as a Tool for Cultivating Critical Consciousness through Elementary English Language Arts and Reading

Kelly C. Johnston

This chapter will introduce *The Day You Begin* as a multicultural tool (Osorio, 2018) to cultivate critical thinking in the content areas of English language arts and reading. *The Day You Begin* offers teachers and children the opportunity to consider perspectives and lived experiences across social, linguistic, and cultural boundaries, a key element of multicultural children's literature (Ghiso, Campano, & Hall, 2012). Indeed, teachers wield great power when choosing texts they will use in their classrooms.

In this lesson, students will examine *difference* through a series of activities. Beginning with a read-aloud, the teacher and students will engage in thoughtful discussion, inquiry, writing, critical reflection, and (for older students) research and action.

BACKGROUND OF THE LITERATURE

The Day You Begin, authored by Jacqueline Woodson—winner of the Coretta Scott King Award (and many more awards) for her renowned work advocating for diversity and inclusion—and illustrated by Rafael López—an internationally known illustrator also awarded for his work celebrating young people of all ethnicities and cultures—thoughtfully features culturally, linguistically, and racially diverse children as they socially experience differences from one another.

Set in a classroom of young children throughout a single school day, each page interweaves children's lived experiences of *difference*. Angelina, a girl of color, hesitantly enters a new class at school, recognizing there is no one who looks quite like her. While the other children tell one another of their summer travels abroad, she must find her voice to tell her story, to boldly speak her name and tell of her summer spent caring for her younger sister.

A young boy from Venezuela, Rigoberto, whose accent sounds unfamiliar to his classmates' ears, must navigate the uncomfortable space of being different and endure the reactions from the children around him. Another young girl's kimchi, meat, and rice lunch draw responses of curiosity and suspicion from new friends. A young boy feels all alone, not picked for teams at recess because he cannot quite keep up.

These children's stories show how they experience loneliness, insecurity, shame, and sadness as a result of being or feeling different from others. Yet, when Angelina shares her summer story with the class, each child's world opens up so that they can better understand one another and make space for the differences that once separated them. They find common ground while growing confidence in the very things that make them unique and different.

The Day You Begin artfully demonstrates the delicate beauty of *humanness* that is often undervalued, discounted, or overlooked both in the classroom and in the world. With a focus on children's lived experiences and their colliding worlds of differences, empathy and appreciation for others are beautifully displayed. The power in these stories highlight *difference* as a human experience to which all children can and should connect.

PEDAGOGICAL APPROACH

Texts, such as children's literature, along with teachers' worldviews and language that reflects those worldviews, shape students' classroom experiences, identity formation, and how they "read the world" (Freire, 1983). Thus, in preparing for this lesson, teachers must first engage in self-reflexivity to consider their own social justice competency (Breunig, 2016): *How do I appreciate others' racial, gender, cultural, and physical differences? What biases do I have toward or against others? Who do I tend to think less or more of depending on these differences? How might others think less of me because of my own differences?* and specifically for pedagogy: *How do I value my students? How can I encourage their identities as an integral part of learning? How can I facilitate opportunities for their voices to be heard and to deepen learning experiences in our class?* Deeply reflecting on these questions better helps one situate one's worldview and guides thoughtful, intentional pedagogical choices for the classroom.

Beyond actively providing children access to diverse textual and illustrative representation in children's literature, teachers have the opportunity to use children's literature as a tool for social justice through cultivating critical consciousness (Osorio, 2018). This is particularly important for multicultural children's literature portraying children's diverse lives.

Osorio outlines key functions of multicultural literature as a tool: (1) Develop an appreciation for diversity, (2) honor students' voices, (3) connect to students' rich linguistic and cultural backgrounds, and (4) promote critical consciousness. Recognizing these specific functions is important for moving beyond simply having multicultural literature in a classroom to using it for strategic purposes.

By introducing *The Day You Begin* with a read-aloud, students engage in personal reflection activities connected to societal problems, which they will explore through writing and research. Through these interrelated activities, students are guided and encouraged to read and think through others' perspectives, an essential component for critically reading multicultural literature with a multicultural lens (Morrell & Morrell, 2012).

This approach also aligns with Osorio's (2018) call to develop an appreciation for diversity. Such appreciation entails moving beyond one's own personal connections to developing an understanding about how someone from a different perspective might interpret a text or a social situation.

Overall, this lesson guides the teacher in culturally responsive teaching that employs a critical stance, an essential aspect of multicultural education (Nieto, 2017). The strategic activities offer opportunities to cultivate critical consciousness and empower the teacher to use the text as a tool (Osorio, 2018).

Such a pedagogical move is not a given, but this lesson, and those that accompany this book, equip the teacher with tangible steps for culturally responsive teaching through multicultural literature (for more on culturally responsive, relevant, affirming, and sustaining teaching, see Gay, 2018; Ladson-Billings, 2009; Paris & Alim, 2017; Scott & Purdum-Cassidy, 2016).

Lesson Objectives (NCTE/IRA, 1996/2012)

- The students will participate as knowledgeable, reflective, creative, and critical members of their classroom literacy community. (elementary, middle, and secondary)
- The students will read a wide range of print and non-print texts to build an understanding of texts, of themselves, and of the cultures of the United States and the world; to acquire new information; to respond to the needs and demands of society and the workplace; and for personal fulfillment. (elementary, middle, and secondary)
- The students will conduct research on issues and interests by generating ideas and questions and by posing problems. They gather, evaluate, and

synthesize data from a variety of sources (e.g., print and non-print texts, artifacts, people) to communicate their discoveries in ways that suit their purpose and audience. (middle and secondary)

Content Overview

In this lesson, students will engage in inquiry-based pedagogical strategies that will stem from a social justice commitment to explore issues of equity and injustice in relation to current events. With this as the overarching theme, teachers and students will engage in critical analysis through dialogic conversations expressed through speaking and writing. Guided questions will be provided to first foster connections to the text and subsequently foster critical consciousness.

Cultivating critical consciousness supports children in critical thinking related to social issues in their worlds (Ladson-Billings, 1995; Osorio, 2018; Souto-Manning, 2009). It is the intentional act of recognizing societal injustices and working toward more equal and just outcomes. Thus, students will engage in self-reflection through writing (mode and format will depend on grade level) as well as critical inquiry through dialogue with one another in relation to social issues and current events (e.g., specific community issues, state issues, or national/international issues such as immigration, discrimination, etc.).

As children examine a social issue of relevance to their lives, they will develop as readers, writers, critical thinkers, and most importantly humans who value the differences in others with appreciation and social action.

Materials/Supplies

- Woodson, J. (2018). *The day you begin.* New York: Nancy Paulsen Books, an imprint of Penguin Random House.
- Interactive display (for example: white board, Smart board, chart paper, or projector)
- Current event articles (either from an online search or a selection of articles printed and organized by the teacher; see Additional Online Resources for more options)
- Writing materials for student responses (paper/pencil, writer's notebook, or online text document)

SEQUENCE OF ACTIVITIES

Elementary

Hook

The teacher will invite students together for a read-aloud. To introduce the book, the teacher will show the cover, read the title and author, and open the book to the introduction of the book jacket. The teacher will read aloud from the book: "There will be times when you walk into a room and no one there is quite like you." The teacher will tell students he or she is going to read this sentence one more time, asking them to consider what it makes them think about. After reading the sentence again, the teacher will invite students to turn and talk to a partner and discuss what they think about this statement (i.e., Can they relate? Have they ever felt different from the people they are around? How so? How did it make them feel?).

Activity No. 1: Read-Aloud

The teacher will tell students he or she is going to read the book aloud. The teacher will ask students to think about the different characters as the book is read aloud, asking students to pay special attention to the ways each character felt different from others. The teacher will then read the book aloud. After reading, the teacher will ask students to turn again to a partner to discuss one of the characters from the read-aloud and how he/she felt different in the book. After students have had two to three minutes to discuss, the teacher will ask if one or two students want to share aloud which character they discussed with their partner and how that character felt different in the story.

Activity No. 2: Examining Connections

The teacher will tell students that this story raised questions that they can think about together. The teacher and students will engage in a whole-group discussion based on the following questions:

- *What differences might each of us feel in our classroom?*
- *What differences do we see in our school? In our community? In our country? In our world?* (Choose one or two contexts that are most appropriate for your students.)

The teacher will think aloud to model a response for the questions. As students respond in their own ways to each question, record their responses so that the whole class can see (e.g., on a white board, Smart board, chart paper, or projector). The teacher will paraphrase their responses to model recording essential information, summarizing, and identifying main ideas. The teacher should take time to hear responses and facilitate discussion on the first question before moving to the second question.

Activity No. 3: Writing for Personal Change

After examining connections, students will engage in a personal writing activity. If possible, the teacher will project the final page of *The Day You Begin* (beginning with "This is the day you begin . . . ") so that all students can see the page. This page will serve as a mentor text for their writing, and the teacher may model an example of the activity while explaining the instructions for the students.

The teacher will explain that students will construct and write their own responses to how they can respond when either feeling different from others or seeing someone else feeling different or left out. Beginning with the sentence stem "This is the day I begin . . . " students will complete the sentence by writing a response to (1) one way they will have confidence when they feel different from others and (2) one way they will think differently (e.g., inclusively, kindly, respectfully) about others who are different from them. Depending on developmental level, students' responses will range (e.g., only completing the sentence stem or writing additional sentences to support their sentence stem response).

Activity No. 4: Reflection for Critical Consciousness

The purpose of this activity is to guide students' personal reflection for critical consciousness. This will look different depending on the students' lived experiences. For students who have been marginalized or oppressed due to differences such as race, gender, or ethnicity, the goal of this activity is to empower them to reflect on systemic inequities that affect their lives and consider how they can respond in a way to change this reality.

For students who have likely experienced privilege due to their racial, ethnic, and socioeconomic backgrounds, the goal of this activity is to help them recognize their privilege and empower them to respond in a way to support those who have been oppressed in ways they have not experienced.[1]

To begin, the teacher will invite students together and remind them about the questions they discussed based on the story. The teacher and students will discuss that all humans have differences (and can refer to particular discussions you had based on the story), which means it is very important people consider how others feel when there are differences and how people respond to big problems because of differences. Using an example based on the group's previous discussion, the teacher will ask students to consider how they can respond to make a difference in the world. The teacher should then use responses to guide a reflection-based discussion.

Middle

Hook

The teacher will select a historical or current event to discuss with the class (see Additional Online Resources section for suggestions). This event should highlight some of the ongoing tensions prevalent in American society that are exacerbated due to human difference (i.e., different perspectives, cultures, worldviews). For example, such an event might relate to specific community, state, or national issues based on immigration (e.g., border policies), racism (e.g., instances of police brutality, the school-to-prison pipeline), or sexism (e.g., biased gender policies in certain institutions). The teachers and students should discuss the possible different perspectives and feelings that led to this event.

Activity No. 1: Read-Aloud

The teacher will tell students that as they continue to think about differences between human beliefs, ideas, and actions, he or she is going to read aloud a children's book to help them think about others' perspectives. Explain that children's books are not only for little children, but that they are for all ages because they often have multiple meanings for all ages. The teacher will ask students to pay close attention to the text, challenging them to think about the deeper messages in the book.

The teacher will then read the book aloud. After reading, the teacher will ask students to turn and talk to a partner to discuss what they think might be some of the deeper messages the author and illustrator hoped to convey to the reader. After students have had two to three minutes to discuss, the teacher will invite one or two students to share aloud.

Activity No. 2: Examining Connections

The teacher will begin by telling students that this story raised questions that they can think about together. Students and teacher will engage in a whole-group discussion based on the following questions:

- *What differences might each of us feel in our classroom?*
- *What differences do we see in our school? In our community? In our country? In our world?* (Choose one or two contexts that are most appropriate for your students.)

The teacher will think aloud to model a response for the questions. As students respond to each question, the teacher will record their responses so that the whole class can see (e.g., on a white board, Smart board, chart paper, or projector). The teacher should paraphrase their responses to model recording essential information, summarizing, and identifying main ideas. The teacher should make time to hear responses and facilitate discussion on the first question before moving to the second question.

Activity No. 3: Writing for Personal Change

After examining connections, students will engage in a personal writing activity. If possible, the teacher will project the final page of *The Day You Begin* (beginning with "This is the day you begin . . . ") so that all students can see the page. This page will serve as a mentor text for their writing, and the teacher may model an example of the activity while ·explaining the instructions for the students. The teacher will ask students to write their own responses to how they can respond when either feeling different from others or seeing someone else feeling different or left out.

Beginning with the sentence stem "This is the day I begin . . . " students will complete the sentence by writing a response to (1) one way they will have confidence when they feel different from others and (2) one way they will think differently (e.g., inclusively, kindly, respectfully) about others who are different from them. Depending on developmental level, students' responses will range (e.g., only completing the sentence stem or writing additional sentences to support their sentence stem response).

Activity No. 4: Researching to Cultivate Critical Consciousness

Cultivating critical consciousness means working to recognize oppressive societal structures and considering what steps one could take to change those structures so that all people are treated fairly and equally. Working independently, in pairs, or in small groups, students will identify one current event that could be approached or framed differently based on the deeper messages conveyed in the earlier reflective discussions from the read-aloud of *The Day You Begin*.

Students will need access to online search engines or to a collection of current event articles already selected by the teacher. Based on their reading of at least two articles on a current event, students should gather, evaluate, and synthesize data to respond to the following guiding questions:

• How can we begin to think about our own personal stories and experiences in relation to this problem?

- Whose point of view is represented in these sources?
- Whose point of view is not represented in these sources?
- What are the main problems discussed in these sources?
- How might a different point of view discuss this problem?
- How have human differences contributed to or alleviated problems related to this topic or event?
- Finally, based on their research, what kind of actions can students take to address the problem in a way that is inclusive of differences? In other words, how might we begin to take action that might create change that brings stories together rather than seeing others' stories as problems?

Students' written responses should follow the format specified by the teacher in accordance with additional standards and expectations.

Activity No. 5: Take Action

Based on their research, students can share their topic and findings with multiple public audiences (class, other classes, school board, community organizations, etc.). An additional step might include students enacting their ideas for change.

Secondary

Hook

The teacher will select a historical or current event to discuss with the class (see Additional Online Resources section for suggestions). This event should highlight some of the ongoing tensions prevalent in American society that are exacerbated due to human difference (i.e., different perspectives, cultures, worldviews). For example, such an event might relate to specific community, state, or national issues based on immigration (e.g., border policies), racism (e.g., instances of police brutality, the school-to-prison pipeline), or sexism (e.g., biased gender policies in certain institutions). The teachers and students should discuss the possible different perspectives and feelings that led to this event.

Activity No. 1: Read-Aloud

The teacher will tell students that as they continue to think about differences between human beliefs, ideas, and actions, he or she is going to read aloud a children's book to help them think about others' perspectives. Explain that children's books are not only for little children, but that they are for all ages because they often have multiple meanings for all ages. The teacher will ask students to pay close attention to the text, challenging them to think about the deeper messages in the book. The teacher will then read the book aloud.

After reading, the teacher will ask students to turn and talk to a partner to discuss what they think might be some of the deeper messages the author and illustrator hoped to convey to the reader. After students have had two to three minutes to discuss, the teacher will invite one or two students to share aloud.

Activity No. 2: Examining Connections

The teacher will begin by telling students that this story raised questions that they can think about together. Students and teacher will engage in a whole-group discussion based on the following questions:

- *What differences might each of us feel in our classroom?*
- *What differences do we see in our school? In our community? In our country? In our world?* (Choose one or two contexts that are most appropriate for your students.)

The teacher will think aloud to model a response for the questions. As students respond to each question, the teacher will record their responses so that the whole class can see (e.g., on a white board, Smart board, chart paper, or projector). The teacher should paraphrase their responses to model recording essential information, summarizing, and identifying main ideas. The teacher should make time to hear responses and facilitate discussion on the first question before moving to the second question.

Activity No. 3: Writing for Personal Change

After examining connections, students will engage in a personal writing activity. If possible, the teacher will project the final page of *The Day You Begin* (beginning with "This is the day you begin . . . ") so that all students can see the page. This page will serve as a mentor text for their writing, and the teacher may model an example of the activity while explaining the instructions for the students. The teacher will ask students to write their own responses to how they can respond when either feeling different from others or seeing someone else feeling different or left out.

Beginning with the sentence stem "This is the day I begin . . . " students will complete the sentence by writing a response to (1) one way they will have confidence when they feel different from others and (2) one way they will think differently (e.g., inclusively, kindly, respectfully) about others who are different from them. Depending on developmental level, students' responses will range (e.g., only completing the sentence stem or writing additional sentences to support their sentence stem response).

Activity No. 4: Researching to Cultivate Critical Consciousness

Cultivating critical consciousness means working to recognize oppressive societal structures and considering what steps one could take to change those structures so that all people are treated fairly and equally. Working independently, in pairs, or in small groups, students will identify one current event that could be approached or framed differently based on the deeper messages conveyed in the earlier reflective discussions from the read-aloud of *The Day You Begin*. Students will need access to online search engines or to a collection of current event articles already selected by the teacher.

Based on their reading of at least two articles on a current event, students should gather, evaluate, and synthesize data to respond to the following guiding questions:

- How can we begin to think about our own personal stories and experiences in relation to this problem?
- Whose point of view is represented in these sources?
- Whose point of view is not represented in these sources?
- What are the main problems discussed in these sources?
- How might a different point of view discuss this problem?
- How have human differences contributed to or alleviated problems related to this topic or event?
- Finally, based on their research, what kind of actions can students take to address the problem in a way that is inclusive of differences? In other words, how might we begin to take action that might create change that brings stories together rather than seeing others' stories as problems?

Students' written responses should follow the format specified by the teacher in accordance with additional standards and expectations.

Activity No. 5: Take Action

Based on their research, students can share their topic and findings with multiple public audiences (class, other classes, school board, community organizations, etc.). The teacher can ask each student, pair, or group where they might share their research to enact public change based on their findings. For example, if students have researched a biased school board policy that has affected students and families at their school, the teacher could support those students in writing a letter to the school board based on their research or presenting at an upcoming school board meeting. This step encourages students to consider how their research not only cultivates critical consciousness for themselves but might also extend to other audiences.

An additional step might include students enacting their ideas for change after publicly sharing findings. For example, if students have researched the issues of homelessness and food scarcity, along with publicly sharing their findings with their local city council and advocating for more community resources and access to these resources, students could organize a food drive for their local shelter or create a free pantry for students at their school.

Tips for Struggling/Reluctant Readers

To differentiate this lesson for reluctant students, consider specific pairing of students based on successful pairing previously experienced in the classroom. Because this lesson heavily draws on students' lived experiences and relationships to one another, it is important all students feel their voices are heard and feel they are in a safe space. The lesson could also be differentiated by using flexible grouping in combination with stations so that activities are offered in smaller groups.

Tips for English Language Learners

In addition to the above tips, this lesson can be differentiated for English Language Leaners (ELLs) by incorporating more discussion and "turn and talk" opportunities during the read-aloud and activities. This collaboration will allow for authentic conversation among students. ELL students may also prefer to engage in writing activities by writing in their first language and then translating to English.

Evaluation of Skills

Evaluation should be based on the lesson objectives. The teacher can use the rubric below to evaluate and provide a detailed response. For example, depending on how a student meets each objective, the teacher will rate the student accordingly by marking either "emerging," "developing," or "proficient" for each objective. The teacher can then provide specific comments in relation to the rating for each objective. This would be especially useful for providing specificity regarding each objective and detailing students' actions that led the teacher to rate at a particular level.

Table 1.1. Rubric to Evaluate Skills

Objective	Emerging	Developing	Proficient
The students will participate as knowledgeable, reflective, creative, and critical members of their classroom literacy community.	The student began to participate in oral discussion, written response, and reflection, demonstrating thinking in response to the activities.	The student actively participated in oral discussion, written response, and reflection, demonstrating thinking in response to the activities.	The student actively participated and suggested new ideas in oral discussion, written response, and reflection, demonstrating thinking in response to the activities.
The students will read a wide range of print and non-print texts to build an understanding of texts, of themselves, and of the cultures of the United States and the world; to acquire new information; to respond to the needs and demands of society and the workplace; and for personal fulfillment.	The student began to read a range of texts to build an understanding of texts, of themselves, and of the cultures of the United States and the world; to acquire new information; to respond to the needs and demands of society and the workplace; and for personal fulfillment.	The student actively read some texts to build an understanding of texts, of themselves, and of the cultures of the United States and the world; to acquire new information; to respond to the needs and demands of society and the workplace; and for personal fulfillment.	The student actively read a wide range of print and non-print texts to build an understanding of texts, of themselves, and of the cultures of the United States and the world; to acquire new information; to respond to the needs and demands of society and the workplace; and for personal fulfillment.
Middle/Secondary: The students will conduct research on issues and interests by generating ideas and questions and by posing problems. They will gather, evaluate, and synthesize data from a variety of sources (e.g., print and non-print texts, artifacts, people) to communicate their discoveries in ways that suit their purpose and audience.	The student began to conduct research on issues and interests by generating ideas and questions and by posing problems. The student is in the initial stages of gathering, evaluating, and synthesizing data to communicate discoveries in ways that suit his/her purpose and audience.	The student is in the process of conducting research on issues and interests by generating ideas and questions and by posing problems. The student is in the process of gathering, evaluating, and synthesizing data to communicate discoveries in ways that suit his/her purpose and audience.	The student actively conducted research on issues and interests by generating ideas and questions and by posing problems. The student actively gathered, evaluated, and synthesized data to communicate discoveries in ways that suited his/her purpose and audience.

ADDITIONAL ONLINE RESOURCES

The following websites may be useful for connecting to current events:

- Scholastic News: scholasticnews.scholastic.com
  Scholastic News provides current event articles for grades 1–6. Along with links to subscribe to a magazine, the website offers free resources organized by grade level.
- News for Kids: newsforkids.net
  News for Kids is a website created by a teacher with the goal of making current events and news accessible for kids. Their motto is "Real news told simply."
- DOGO News: www.dogonews.com
  DOGO News offers articles organized by content, such as science, social studies, world, and environment. These articles are hyperlinked by key words, offer a listening option, and provide students with options to respond to questions, comment on the article, and interact online with others.
- Time for Kids: www.timeforkids.com
  Time for Kids provides current event news articles organized online by grade level. These articles are written in alignment with the Common Core State Standards as well.

CONCLUDING REMARKS

Cultivating critical consciousness is a necessary element of critical thinking, especially in equipping students with the cognitive skills to actively engage in social change to make our world a more equitable and just place for all people. Such a stance on life and social events takes time, patience, and critical reflection. This lesson began with implications for teachers to ready themselves before teaching the lesson.

Teachers should take time to consider their biases, viewpoints, and beliefs (based on the suggested questions in the "Pedagogical Approach" section) as well as anticipating how students might respond to such questions. Teachers should also consider the classroom culture regarding how students engage in conversations that might elicit different opinions or cause some discomfort. For example, teachers and students could establish a respectful format for responses to classmates when participating in group discussion, such as choosing from sentence stems such as "I understand that you think . . . , but I also think . . . " to frame differences of opinion.

Additionally, as teachers facilitate the activities and plan to assess with the rubric, they can flexibly incorporate other English language arts and reading standards and objectives as needed. For example, if students have also been focusing on sequencing the order of events as an ELAR skill, teachers can incorporate this when examining current events with students. This could be done through a mini-activity the teacher brings into the lesson activities in either whole-group, small-group, or independent format.

NOTE

1. Oppression refers to the systemic or organized ways certain groups have been marginalized in society.

REFERENCES

Breunig, M. (2016). Critical and social justice pedagogies in practice. In M. Peters (ed.), *Encyclopedia of educational philosophy and theory*, 978–981. New York: Springer.

Freire, P. (1983). The importance of the act of reading. *Journal of education*, *165*(1), 5–11.

Gay, G. (2018). *Culturally responsive teaching: Theory, research, and practice.* Multicultural Education Series. New York: Teachers College Press.

Ghiso, M., Campano, G., & Hall, T. (2012). Braided histories and experiences in literature for children and adolescents. *Journal of Children's Literature*, *38*(2), 14–22.

Ladson-Billings, G. (1995). But that's just good teaching! The case for culturally relevant pedagogy. *Theory into practice*, *34*(3), 159–165.

Ladson-Billings, G. (2009). *The dreamkeepers: Successful teachers of African American children.* San Francisco, CA: John Wiley & Sons.

Morrell, E., & Morrell, J. (2012). Multicultural readings of multicultural literature and the promotion of social awareness in ELA classrooms. *New England Reading Association Journal, 47*(2), 10–16, 81.

National Council of Teachers of English/International Reading Association. (1996/2012). *Standards for the English language arts.* Retrieved from ncte.org/standards/ncteira.

Nieto, S. (2017). Re-imagining multicultural education: New visions, new possibilities. *Multicultural Education Review*, *9*(1), 1–10.

Osorio, S. L. (2018). Multicultural literature as a classroom tool. *Multicultural Perspectives, 20*(1), 47–52.

Paris, D., & Alim, H. S. (Eds.). (2017). *Culturally sustaining pedagogies: Teaching and learning for justice in a changing world.* New York: Teachers College Press.

Scott, L., & Purdum-Cassidy, B. (Eds.). (2016). *Culturally affirming literacy practices for urban elementary students.* Lanham, MD: Rowan & Littlefield.

Souto-Manning, M. (2009). Negotiating culturally responsive pedagogy through multicultural children's literature: Towards critical democratic literacy practices in a first-grade classroom. *Journal of Early Childhood Literacy*, *9*(1), 50–74.

Woodson, J. (2018). *The Day You Begin*. New York: Nancy Paulsen Books, an imprint of Penguin Random House.

2

Separate Is Never Equal

Utilizing Question-Answer Relationships to Foster Students' Reading Comprehension

Elena M. Venegas

This chapter presents lessons for the English language arts and reading classroom using the Question-Answer Relationships (QAR) strategy with the book *Separate Is Never Equal: Sylvia Mendez and Her Family's Fight for Desegregation*. Both the book and the lessons presented center on historical and contemporary issues surrounding school segregation, desegregation, and resegregation. Thus, the lessons presented in this chapter are also appropriate for the social studies classroom and may be used to address curriculum standards set forth by the National Council for the Social Studies.

Through its use of both explicit and implicit questioning, the Question-Answer Relationships strategy can be utilized to help students prepare for the types of questions that they may encounter on standardized examinations. *Separate Is Never Equal* and the lessons that follow celebrate the accomplishments of people of color and linguistically diverse peoples in enacting societal change within the United States.

BACKGROUND OF THE LITERATURE

Duncan Tonatiuh authored *Separate Is Never Equal: Sylvia Mendez and Her Family's Fight for Desegregation*. Tonatiuh tells the lesser-known story of Sylvia Mendez, whose family's fight to end school segregation proceeded the landmark *Brown v. Board of Education* (1954) U.S. Supreme Court decision, which mandated school integration.

In 1944, the aunt of Sylvia Mendez attempted to enroll her own daughters along with Sylvia and her brothers in school in Westminster, California. The secretary informed Sylvia's aunt that her daughters could enroll but that the

Mendez children had to enroll in "the Mexican school" (Tonatiuh, 2014, p. 8). Sylvia wondered if her cousins could attend the Westminster school because of their fair skin, light-colored hair, and French surname.

As her niece and nephews faced colorism, Aunt Soledad did not enroll any of the children in the Westminster school. Instead, the children attended "the Mexican school" (Tonatiuh, 2014, p. 15). The facilities and quality of education offered to the Latinx students were inferior to those offered to white students, which reflected the perception of students of color held by district administrators. However, the Mendez family refused to accept the status quo.

Separate Is Never Equal can be used to discuss historic school segregation with elementary students through the lens of young children such as Sylvia Mendez and Ruby Bridges. *Separate Is Never Equal* is a springboard for discussing resistance to school desegregation as well as researching school (de)segregation within local communities at the middle school level.

For secondary students, the book serves as a catalyst for discussing the resegregation of contemporary schools. The rich resources included at the end of the book are tools that can enhance these lessons. For example, the author's note on pages 36–37 features photos of the Mendez family and elaborates on their story while also addressing contemporary school segregation.

Other helpful resources in the book include a glossary, a bibliography of resources utilized by Tonatiuh to inform the book, and an index. These resources can help the reader to define terms, conduct further research, and easily locate information within the text. Finally, the Spanish language is interspersed throughout *Separate Is Never Equal*. An English translation immediately follows Spanish sentences. For example, "No queremos problemas" precedes the English translation, "We don't want any problems" (Tonatiuh, 2014, p. 17). The inclusion of the Spanish language enhances the authenticity of the book, given its focus on Latinx characters, and may particularly resonate with Spanish-speaking readers.

PEDAGOGICAL APPROACH

This chapter recommends utilizing Question-Answer Relationships (QAR) to facilitate students' reading comprehension of *Separate Is Never Equal* in the English language arts and reading classroom. However, the lessons presented below are closely related to social studies and could be used to address the National Curriculum Standards for Social Studies.

Separate Is Never Equal as well as the lessons presented below focus on historical segregation and could be used to address Standard 2, "Social studies programs should include experiences that provide for the study of the past and its legacy" (National Council for the Social Studies, n.d., n.p.). The book and lessons focused on the fight to desegregate schools could address Standards 6 and 10.

Standard 6 focuses on societal changes and states, "Social studies programs should include experiences that provide for the study of how people create, interact with, and change structures of power, authority, and governance" (National Council for the Social Studies, n.d., n.p.). Similarly, Standard 10 states, "Social studies programs should include experiences that provide for the study of the ideals, principles, and practices of citizenship in a democratic republic" (National Council for the Social Studies, n.d., n.p.).

Raphael (1986) developed QAR, a reading comprehension strategy that requires students to answer both explicit and implicit questions. QAR can be taught to students as a test preparation strategy as it reflects the types of questions they will encounter on standardized examinations (Green, 2016). Several reading comprehension strategies are accessed via QAR such as (1) activating prior knowledge, (2) making connections, (3) recognizing text features, (4) summarizing, (5) visualizing, (6) clarifying, and (7) inferring (Raphael & Au, 2005).

QAR is a versatile strategy that is appropriate across disciplines, including mathematics (McIntosh & Draper, 1995), science (Kinniburgh & Baxter, 2012), and social studies (Ouzts, 1998). To use the Question-Answer Relationships strategy, a teacher should first preview the corresponding text(s). Then teachers can write one of four types of questions that fall into two categories: explicit questions and implicit questions.

The first type of explicit question is categorized as "Right There" (Raphael, 1986, p. 518), the answer to which is directly stated in the text. "Think and Search" questions (Raphael, 1986, p. 518) are also explicit questions yet task students with synthesizing information presented throughout the text. The second category of questions are implicit. "Author and You" questions (Raphael, 1986, p. 518) are implicit in that students must utilize their own background knowledge coupled with the text to answer them, whereas students can answer "On My Own" questions (Raphael, 1986, p. 518) solely using their own background knowledge.

When introducing QAR to students, it is important for teachers to first communicate the objectives of the lesson, model the strategy while verbalizing related terminology (e.g., Right There question, Author and You question), and engage students in guided practice before expecting them to independently use the QAR strategy (Fenty, McDuffie-Landrum, & Fisher, 2012).

Introduce an anchor chart depicting the two categories of questions and the two question types within each category to students when modeling QAR. Students will find this anchor chart especially useful as they begin to use

QAR independently. Social understanding, or understanding and sympathizing with others, may be built through reading (Kozak & Recchia, 2018). Thus, reading multicultural children's literature such as *Separate Is Never Equal* has the potential to foster students' social understanding of diverse peoples and/or cultural groups.

Furthermore, a study conducted by May (2010) suggested that strategies that engage students in making connections, visualizing, and inferring align well with culturally relevant teaching. These strategies, as previously mentioned, are among several reading comprehension strategies utilized in QAR. *Separate Is Never Equal* may particularly resonate with students of color whose predecessors faced racially and/or ethnically based segregation not only in the South but also in other regions of the United States.

Linguistically diverse students may connect with the language discrimination presented in the book. For example, the Westminster School District superintendent claimed to send Latinx children "to the Mexican school to help them improve their English" (Tonatiuh, 2014, p. 25). The lesson activities presented below use *Separate Is Never Equal* to facilitate conversations about school segregation and desegregation. Such conversations are also intended to foster respect for racial and/or ethnic diversity.

Lesson Objectives

- "Students read a wide range of print and nonprint texts to build an understanding of texts, of themselves, and of the cultures of the United States and the world; to acquire new information; to respond to the needs and demands of society and the workplace; and for personal fulfillment. Among these texts are fiction and nonfiction, classic and contemporary works" (International Reading Association & National Council of Teachers of English, 1996, p. 19).
- "Students apply a wide range of strategies to comprehend, interpret, evaluate, and appreciate texts. They draw on their prior experience, their interactions with other readers and writers, their knowledge of word meaning and of other texts, their word identification strategies, and their understanding of textual features (e.g., sound-letter correspondence, sentence structure, context, graphics)" (International Reading Association & National Council of Teachers of English, 1996, p. 22).
- "Students conduct research on issues and interests by generating ideas and questions, and by posing problems. They gather, evaluate, and synthesize data from a variety of sources (e.g., print and nonprint texts, artifacts, people) to communicate their discoveries in ways that suit their purpose and audience" (International Reading Association & National Council of Teachers of English, 1996, p. 27).

- "Students use a variety of technological and informational resources (e.g., libraries, databases, computer networks, video) to gather and synthesize information and to create and communicate knowledge" (International Reading Association & National Council of Teachers of English, 1996, p. 28).
- "Students develop an understanding of and respect for diversity in language use, patterns, and dialects across cultures, ethnic groups, geographic regions, and social roles" (International Reading Association & National Council of Teachers of English, 1996, p. 29).

Content Overview

This lesson uses QAR with *Separate Is Never Equal* to foster a discussion about social issues such as racism, colorism, prejudice, and discrimination through questioning. For example, answering the Right There questions in Table 2.1 below can lead to a discussion of colorism. Colorism "centers on advantages and disadvantages of people who identify as the same race experience based on the lightness or darkness of their skin tone, and other external traits" (Keith & Monroe, 2016, p. 4).

Answering Think and Search questions, such as the one presented in Table 2.1, requires students to reflect on the book in its entirety as well as provide evidence from the text to support their assertions. The Author and You question presented in Table 2.1 requires the use of the text and students' background knowledge. Answering this question may lead to a discussion of how the victory of one group of students of color (e.g., Latinx students) extended to *all* students of color.

Table 2.1.   Examples of Questions for Usage with Question-Answer Relationships (QAR)

Question	Type of Question-Answer Relationship
Why were Sylvia and her brothers denied admission into the Westminster school while their cousins were not?	Right There
On what basis did the school district superintendents deny students of color admission into the white schools such as the Westminster school?	Think and Search
Why did other racially and ethnically based organizations such as the National Association for the Advancement of Colored People (NAACP) write letters of support to the judges on the Court of Appeals?	Author and You
How has school integration affected the United States?	On My Own

On My Own questions, such as the one presented in Table 2.1, require students to rely solely on their prior knowledge. For elementary students, the primary focus of the lesson is on the *Mendez v. Westminster* case itself; however, the last activity connects the case with the larger nationwide fight against school desegregation.

For middle school students, *Separate Is Never Equal* serves as a spring-board for research into resistance to school desegregation as well as research into the impact of school segregation and desegregation upon local communities.

After reading *Separate Is Never Equal*, secondary students will explore audio and video resources that present a historical view of desegregation as well as argue that American schools have become resegregated. Students will then research in preparation to debate whether contemporary schools are desegregated but not integrated or both integrated and desegregated.

Materials/Supplies

- Above the Noise. (2018). *Why are schools still segregated?* Retrieved from www.youtube.com/watch?v=v2TG9n0vc-4&feature=youtu.be
- Anchor chart depicting Question-Answer Relationships
- Bell, Debra. (2013). George Wallace stood in a doorway at the University of Alabama 50 years ago today. *U.S. News & World Report.* Retrieved from www.usnews.com/news/blogs/press-past/2013/06/11/george-wallace-stood-in-a-doorway-at-the-university-of-alabama-50-years-ago-today
- Computer with Internet access and connected projector
- iPad/tablet with Internet access and headphones/earbuds
- National Public Radio. (2014). *Nearly six decades later, integration remains a work in progress.* Retrieved from listenwise.com/current_events/159-racial-integration-in-little-rock-decades-later
- National Public Radio. (2003). *Wallace in the schoolhouse door.* Retrieved from listenwise.com/lessons/286-george-wallace-at-the-school-door
- Photographs of the following historical figures: young Felicitas Mendez (Sylvia's mom), older Felicitas Mendez, young Sylvia Mendez, adult Sylvia Mendez, young Gonzalo Mendez (Sylvia's dad), David Marcus (attorney), Paul J. McCormick (federal judge), young Thurgood Marshall (attorney), Linda Brown of *Brown v. Board of Education*, Earl Warren (California governor), older Thurgood Marshall (Supreme Court justice), older Earl Warren (chief justice of the Supreme Court)

- Question-Answer Relationships (QAR) graphic organizer (two per student)
- Scholastic. (2018). *Ruby Bridges and the Civil Rights Movement slide show for grades K–2*. Retrieved from www.scholastic.com/teachers/slideshows/teaching-content/ruby-bridges-and-the-civil-rights-movement-slide-show-for-kinder/
- Scholastic. (2018). *Ruby Bridges and the Civil Rights Movement slide show teaching guide, kindergarten to grade 2*. Retrieved from www.scholastic.com/teachers/articles/teaching-content/ruby-bridges-and-civil-rights-movement-slide-show-teaching-guide-kindergarten-grade-2/#tech-tips
- Tonatiuh, Duncan. (2014). *Separate is never equal: Sylvia Mendez and her family's fight for desegregation*. New York: Abrams Books for Young Readers.
- Administrative Office of the U.S. Courts. (2018). *Script—Mendez v. Westminster re-enactment*. Retrieved from www.uscourts.gov/educational-resources/educational-activities/script-mendez-v-westminster-re-enactment
- WBUR News. (2018). *How the Boston busing decision still affects city schools 40 years later*. Retrieved from www.wbur.org/news/2014/06/20/boston-busing-ruling-anniversary
- Writing utensil (one per student)

SEQUENCE OF ACTIVITIES

Elementary

Hook

The teacher will open the lesson with a hook to engage students by stating, "How would you feel if someone told you that you could no longer go to [name of school] because of your hair color? Instead, you must go to a school built especially for students with your hair color. Only your school is not as nice as the school for students with other colored hair. Your school is dirty and smelly and does not have any materials to enhance your learning. [Solicit students' reactions, thoughts, and feelings to the presented scenario.]

"Before 1954, it was legal for schools to be segregated, and students were often separated based on the color of their skin. Today, we are going to read *Separate Is Never Equal* by Duncan Tonatiuh, which tells the story about one family's fight against school segregation."

Activity No. 1: Teacher Read-Aloud and QAR Strategy

Separate Is Never Equal has a Lexile level of AD870L, which is at the reading level of grade 4 through grade 6 students, although recommended to be read by and/or with an adult. Thus, the teacher will first conduct a whole class read-aloud of the text.

The book is quite lengthy so the teacher may need to read it over the course of several days, depending on the students' grade level. Use the anchor chart (see example in Table 2.2 below) to introduce the QAR strategy to students in teacher-directed small groups wherein students will meet to apply the strategy to the book.

Table 2.2.   Question-Answer Relationships (QAR) Anchor Chart

Explicit questions	Implicit questions
Right There	Author and You
The answer is directly stated in the text.	Use your background knowledge and the text to answer this question.
Think and Search	On My Own
The answer is stated across several sentences, paragraphs, and/or pages.	Answer this question using your background knowledge.

Be sure to use strategy-related terminology (e.g., On My Own question) as you model for students how to determine the answer to one of four questions (see examples in Figure 2.1 below) and identify the type of question-answer relationship. Model for students how to complete the Question-Answer Relationships (QAR) graphic organizer for the first question.

Engage students in guided practice by answering two other questions, identifying the types of question-answer relationships, and completing the related sections of the graphic organizer. Finally, students will answer the last question as independent practice, identify the type of question-answer relationship, and complete the corresponding section of the graphic organizer on their own.

Activity No. 2: Reenacting Sylvia Mendez's Story

As a class, students will reenact Sylvia Mendez's story. The script (i.e., *Script—Mendez v. Westminster re-enactment*) features prominent persons involved in the *Mendez v. Westminster* case, including Mendez family members, attorney David Marcus, (later U.S. Supreme Court justice) Earl Warren, and others. Prior to performing the reenactment, assign each student the role of one prominent figure. The roles of narrator and greeter must also be filled. As each figure speaks about his or her role in the *Mendez v. Westminster* case, another student will hold up a historical photograph of that person.

Question	Answer	Type of Question-Answer Relationship
Why were Sylvia and her brothers denied admission into the Westminster school while their cousins were not?		*Right There* Think and Search Author and You On My Own
On what basis did the school district superintendents deny students of color admission into the White schools such as Westminster school?		Right There *Think and Search* Author and You On My Own
Why did other race- and ethnically-based organizations such as the National Association for the Advancement of Colored People (NAACP) write letters of support to the judges on the Court of Appeals?		Right There Think and Search *Author and You* On My Own
How has school integration affected the United States?		Right There Think and Search Author and You *On My Own*

Figure 2.1.   QAR Graphic Organizer Using *Separate is Never Equal*

This reenactment could be performed within the classroom, for other students, or for the students' families. The purpose of this reenactment is to extend students' knowledge of the role each person played not only in the Mendez case but in advancing civil rights in California and the United States at large.

Activity No. 3: Connecting the Experiences of Sylvia Mendez and Ruby Bridges

The purpose of connecting Sylvia Mendez's experience to that of Ruby Bridges is to expand students' understanding that school segregation was a problem across the United States and was not unique to California or to Latinx students. This will be accomplished through a whole class lesson using a slideshow featuring historical photographs from the civil rights era and of Ruby Bridges, an African American girl who integrated a previously all-white school.

First, read the accompanying teaching guide (i.e., *Ruby Bridges and the Civil Rights Movement Slide Show Teaching Guide, Kindergarten to Grade* 2) to become familiar or reacquainted with the historical content presented in the slideshow. Then present the slideshow (i.e., *Ruby Bridges and the Civil Rights Movement Slide Show for Grades K–2*) to the class.

Based on students' previous success and familiarity with QAR, students will work either independently or with a partner to complete a Question-Answer Relationships (QAR) graphic organizer applicable to both the book (i.e., *Separate Is Never Equal*) and the slideshow (i.e., *Ruby Bridges and the Civil Rights Movement Slide Show for Grades K–2*).

Students will answer each question that you pose as well as determine the type of question-answer relationship for each question. Completion of this graphic organizer will be used as a means of formative assessment to determine (a) students' understanding of school segregation and integration and (b) students' application of the QAR strategy.

Middle

Hook

The teacher will open the lesson with a hook to engage students by stating, "Did you know that schools in our state (or a neighboring state or in the South) used to be segregated? School segregation was based on the U.S. Supreme Court decision *Plessy v. Ferguson* (1896), which stated that segregation was acceptable if facilities were 'separate but equal.' In terms of schools, this meant that some were designated as all-white schools whereas others were created specifically for African American students or Latinx students. Although the law stated that schools and other institutions could be segregated based on race and/or ethnicity, the institutions that served whites were often far superior to those that served people of color.

"Therefore, people of color were not treated equally to whites. Today, you are going to read *Separate Is Never Equal* authored by Duncan Tonatiuh. In the book, Tonatiuh describes the poor conditions of a 'Mexican school' in California attended by Sylvia Mendez and other Latinx children. Tonatiuh

Question	Answer	Type of Question-Answer Relationship
Slide 1		Right There
Was school segregation limited to California? If not, in what region was school segregation primarily concentrated?		Think and Search (Author and You) On My Own (This question can be answered the *Ruby Bridges and the Civil Rights Movement slide show for grades K-2* and the students' knowledge, acquired previously from reading *Separate is Never Equal*)
Slide 5		Right There
What were some similarities between the African-American schools in the South and the Mexican-American schools in California? How did the African-American and Mexican-American schools differ from the White schools?		(Think and Search) Author and You On My Own (This question requires students to synthesize information presented in both the book and the slideshow.)
Slide 6		(Right There)
How was the *Brown v. Board of Education* (1954) Supreme		Think and Search Author and You

Figure 2.2.   QAR Graphic Organizer for Elementary Students Using Ruby Bridges Slideshow

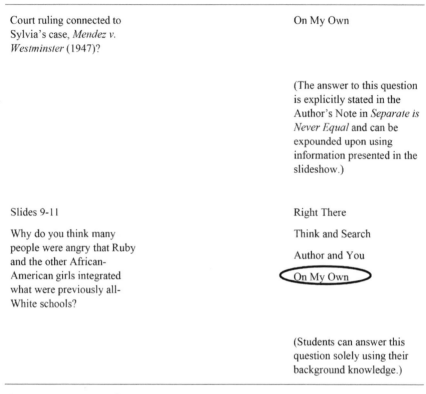

Court ruling connected to   On My Own
Sylvia's case, *Mendez v.*
Westminster (1947)?

                                   (The answer to this question
                                   is explicitly stated in the
                                   Author's Note in *Separate is*
                                   Never Equal and can be
                                   expounded upon using
                                   information presented in the
                                   slideshow.)

Slides 9-11   Right There

Why do you think many   Think and Search
people were angry that Ruby
                                   Author and You
and the other African-
American girls integrated   On My Own
what were previously all-
White schools?

                                   (Students can answer this
                                   question solely using their
                                   background knowledge.)

Figure 2.2.   *(continued)*

then describes the *Mendez v. Westminster* court case, which challenged school segregation in California."

Activity No. 1: Paired Reading and QAR Strategy

While the readability level of *Separate Is Never Equal* is appropriate for most middle school students, reading the book in pairs may be helpful, especially for students who may read dysfluently. First, rank-order students based on their current grade-equivalent reading levels (e.g., seventh grade) and their fluency rates (e.g., 180 words correct per minute). Next, divide the list in half and pair students accordingly. For example, in a class of ten students, #1 is paired with #6 whereas #5 is paired with #10.

This approach ensures that the less fluent reader receives scaffolded support, if needed, from his or her partner while ideally preventing the more fluent reader from becoming frustrated with his or her partner. After a paired reading of *Separate Is Never Equal*, students will continue to work with partners to complete the Question-Answer Relationships (QAR) graphic organizer (see example in Figure 2.1). Be sure to display the QAR anchor chart (Table 2.2) for students to refer to as they complete the graphic organizer.

To ensure that students have correctly applied the QAR strategy, call on random pairs of students to share their answer to each question as well as provide the type of question-answer relationship behind each question. (Note: This activity assumes that students were previously introduced to QAR. If students are unfamiliar with QAR, please see Elementary, Activity 1 for a guide on how to introduce the strategy.)

Activity No. 2: Resistance to School Desegregation

Just as Westminster School resisted school desegregation in the Mendez case, school desegregation was met with resistance across the United States. Despite the favorable U.S. Supreme Court ruling of *Brown v. Board of Education* (1954), many academic institutions continued to be segregated and had to be forcibly integrated.

Independently, each student will read Bell's (2013) article "George Wallace Stood in a Doorway at the University of Alabama 50 Years Ago Today." This article is unique in that Bell writes of resistance to school desegregation from a contemporary perspective. However, the article also includes the historical perspective through photographs and snippets of articles published during 1963, at the time of these tumultuous events, in *U.S. News & World Report*.

Reading this article provides students with greater insight into the historical perspective of school desegregation. After reading Bell's article, each student will complete the Question-Answer Relationships (QAR) graphic organizer (see Figure 2.3). This graphic organizer will be collected as a means of formative assessment to determine (a) students' understanding of resistance to school desegregation and (b) students' application of the QAR strategy.

Activity No. 3: School Segregation and Desegregation in the Community

For this activity, students will work in small groups to research the impact of school segregation and desegregation in a community. Ideally, students will research their own or a neighboring community, if applicable. Students can interview family and/or community members who experienced school segregation and/or desegregation. Students can also visit the local library to access related newspaper articles and/or other media resources published during that time. The Internet and other online resources can also serve as sources of information.

Question	Answer	Type of Question-Answer Relationship
Why do you think that the majority of African-American students in the South attended higher education institutions known as Historically Black Colleges and Universities, such as Tuskegee Institute, during this era?		Right There Think and Search ⟨Author and You⟩ On My Own (This question can be answered using Bell's (2013) article and students' prior knowledge.)
How did the federal government respond to states who resisted school desegregation? Why did the federal government respond in this way?		Right There ⟨Think and Search⟩ Author and You On My Own (This question requires students to synthesize information presented throughout Bell's (2013) article.)
Who was President of the United States during this era, and what was political support for desegregation like during this era?		⟨Right There⟩ Think and Search Author and You On My Own

Figure 2.3.   QAR Graphic Organizer for Middle School Students Using Bell's (2013) Article

<table>
<tr><td></td><td>(The answers to these questions are explicitly stated in Bell's (2013) article.)</td></tr>
<tr><td>Who were some of the leaders of the Civil Rights Movement who helped to champion the cause of African-Americans and other people of color?</td><td>Right There

Think and Search

Author and You

On My Own</td></tr>
<tr><td></td><td>(Students can answer this question solely using their background knowledge.)</td></tr>
</table>

If school segregation was not an issue in the local community, then students can identify a community whose school desegregation was well-publicized (e.g., Little Rock, Arkansas—Little Rock Nine; Topeka, Kansas—Linda Brown of *Brown v. Board of Education*; Oxford, Mississippi—James Meredith at University of Mississippi). Again, students can use the Internet and other online resources to inform their research. Students can likewise visit the library to gather other sources of information. Present your students with questions to guide their research such as:

• What were schools in (selected community) like at the time of segregation?
• What efforts were made to desegregate schools in (selected community)?
• Who were the individuals, groups, and/or organizations that played a role in desegregating the schools in (selected community)?
• How did the people of (selected community) respond to efforts to desegregate their community schools?
• When were schools in (selected community) ultimately desegregated?
• How did the desegregation of schools impact (selected community)?

Students will then present their research before the class, school, and/or families via a multimedia presentation. Use a rubric to evaluate each group's presentation.

Secondary

Hook

The teacher will open the lesson with a hook to engage students by stating, "Segregation found its legal basis in the U.S. Supreme Court ruling, *Plessy v. Ferguson* (1896), which stated that whites and people of color could be segregated so long as their facilities were 'separate but equal.' Prior to the 1954 U.S. Supreme Court ruling in the case of *Brown v. Board of Education*, therefore, students could legally be segregated into separate schools based on their race and/or ethnicity. Although it is now against the law for schools to be segregated, many argue that schools are more segregated now than they were prior to 1954.

"Today, you are going to read *Separate Is Never Equal* authored by Duncan Tonatiuh. In the book, Tonatiuh describes how Sylvia Mendez and other Latinx families challenged school segregation in California. This book will serve as a basis for research into historical and contemporary school segregation in the United States."

Activity No. 1: Independent Reading and QAR Strategy

The readability level of the book *Separate Is Never Equal* makes it appropriate for most high school students to read the book independently. After independently reading *Separate Is Never Equal*, students will continue to work individually to complete the Question-Answer Relationships (QAR) graphic organizer (see example in Table 2.3). Be sure to display the QAR anchor chart (Table 2.2) for students to refer to as they complete the graphic organizer.

To ensure that students have correctly applied the QAR strategy, call on random students to share their answer to each question as well as provide the type of question-answer relationship behind each question. (Note: This activity assumes that students were previously introduced to QAR. If students are unfamiliar with QAR, please see Elementary, Activity 1 for a guide on how to introduce the strategy.)

Activity No. 2: Contemporary Schools: Desegregated or Integrated?

The second learning activity tasks students with accessing three media files related to historic school desegregation and the contemporary resegregation of schools in many American communities. Using an iPad/tablet with Internet access and headphones/earbuds, students should independently watch the video *Why Are Schools Still So Segregated?* by Above the Noise (2018).

Students will also listen to an audio file, *Nearly Six Decades Later, Integration Remains a Work in Progress*, produced by National Public Radio (2014). Finally, students should listen to another audio file, *How the Boston Busing Decision Still Affects City Schools 40 Years Later*, produced by WBUR News (2014).

After watching the video and listening to both audio files, each student will complete the Question-Answer Relationships (QAR) graphic organizer (see Figure 2.4). This graphic organizer will be collected as a means of formative assessment to determine (a) students' understanding of school desegregation and resegregation and (b) students' application of the QAR strategy.

Question	Answer	Type of Question-Answer Relationship
Video: *Why are schools still so segregated?*		⟨Right There⟩
		Think and Search
		Author and You
What is cross-district bussing? What is the phenomenon known as "White flight"?		On My Own
		(The answers to these questions are explicitly stated in the video by Above the Noise (2018).)
Audio: *Nearly six decades later, integration remains a work in progress*		Right There
		⟨Think and Search⟩
		Author and You
		On My Own
Why do contemporary students at Central High School claim to be desegregated but not integrated?		(This question requires students to synthesize information presented in the audio file published by National Public Radio, Inc. (2014, January 13).)

Figure 2.4.   QAR Graphic Organizer for Secondary School Students Using Media Files

Elena M. Venegas

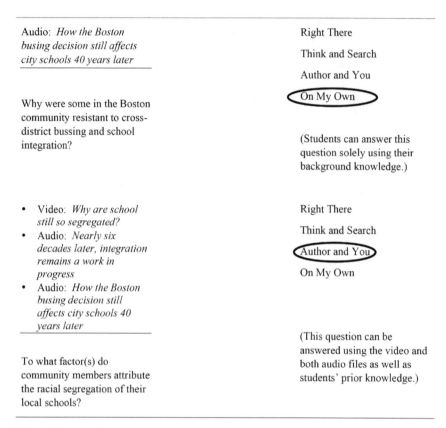

Audio: *How the Boston busing decision still affects city schools 40 years later*	Right There Think and Search Author and You (On My Own)
Why were some in the Boston community resistant to cross-district bussing and school integration?	(Students can answer this question solely using their background knowledge.)
• Video: *Why are school still so segregated?* • Audio: *Nearly six decades later, integration remains a work in progress* • Audio: *How the Boston busing decision still affects city schools 40 years later*	Right There Think and Search (Author and You) On My Own
To what factor(s) do community members attribute the racial segregation of their local schools?	(This question can be answered using the video and both audio files as well as students' prior knowledge.)

Figure 2.4. *(continued)*

Activity No. 3: Research and Debate

As a cumulative activity, divide the class in half to prepare for an in-class debate. One-half of the class will argue that contemporary schools are merely legally desegregated (but not integrated) whereas the other half of the class will argue that contemporary schools are integrated (and desegregated).

In preparation for the debate, students will need to conduct research in order to cite evidence from credible sources that support the position to which they were assigned. Students can visit the school and/or community library as well as use the Internet to conduct their research.

The class will then engage in an in-class debate with each side arguing the merit(s) of their assigned position. The winner of the debate could be determined by either (a) the teacher, (b) a majority vote by the students, or (c) an outside panel consisting of other teachers, administrators, community members, and so on.

Tips for Struggling/Reluctant Readers

Students for whom reading can be challenging will benefit from additional time to read *Separate Is Never Equal*. By receiving the book in advance, students could read it with a teacher, paraprofessional/tutor, or at home with a family member. Reading can be a challenge for approximately 80% of students with learning disabilities (Levine & Wagner, 2003), and these students particularly benefit from the same strategy being reinforced across their classes (Biancarosa & Snow, 2006).

Utilizing QAR in other discipline-related classes (e.g., mathematics, science, social studies) helps students internalize the strategy for independent use and become more proficient in applying it to a variety of texts. Students who find reading challenging may also benefit from a personal-sized version of the QAR anchor chart, which can be kept at their desks, to facilitate their application of the strategy. The following are means of differentiating the lesson for unique activities.

- Elementary, Activity 2: Provide students for whom reading is challenging with the reenactment script in advance. This will allow these students to have additional time to read and practice the speech with a teacher, paraprofessional/tutor, and/or family member at home.
- Middle, Activity 1: This activity already provides differentiation for students for whom reading is challenging as students will be assigned a partner with whom to read *Separate Is Never Equal*. When partnered appropriately, each student for whom reading is a challenge can receive scaffolding from his or her partner.
- Middle, Activity 3 and Secondary, Activity 3: Encourage students to use an array of print and non-print texts as they conduct their research. Students should not be discouraged from reading texts that are either below or above their current grade level.

Tips for English Learners

Regardless of grade level, English learners can listen to an audio version of *Separate Is Never Equal* to enhance their comprehension of the text. (Note: The audio CD is listed in the Additional Online Resources section.) Following along with the audiobook while reading the printed version can resolve any unknown words that English learners may encounter as well as model the pronunciation of such words.

To complete the second QAR graphic organizer (i.e., Elementary, Activity 3—Figure 2.2; Middle, Activity 2—Figure 2.3; Secondary, Activity 2—Figure 2.4), each English learner can be paired with a student who is bilingual in both English and the English learner's first language or with a native English speaker. The following are means of differentiating the lesson for unique activities.

- Elementary, Activity 2: Provide English learners who were selected for one of the reenactment roles with the corresponding script in advance. This will allow English learners to have additional time to practice the speech with the teacher, paraprofessional/tutor, and/or family member at home.
- Middle, Activity 2: For this activity, English learners can listen to the audio file, *Wallace in the Schoolhouse Door*, using an iPad/tablet with Internet access and headphones/earbuds.
- Secondary, Activity 2: English learners can read the transcript of the audio file, *How the Boston Busing Decision Still Affects City Schools 40 Years Later*.

Evaluation of Skills

- Lesson objective 1: To evaluate students' synthesis of information from various print and non-print texts, teachers can rely upon students' completed Question-Answer Relationships (QAR) graphic organizers. (See evaluation of lesson objective 2 below.) Additionally, middle school teachers can evaluate students' small group presentations whereas secondary teachers can evaluate their students' in-class debates. (For both activities, see evaluation of lesson objective 3 below.)
- Lesson objective 2: To evaluate students' application of the QAR strategy, collect the second QAR graphic organizer that students completed. For elementary students, this QAR graphic organizer (i.e., Figure 2.2) was based on *Ruby Bridges and the Civil Rights Movement Slide Show for Grades K–2* and completed either independently or with a partner during Activity 3. For middle school students, this QAR graphic organizer (i.e., Figure 2.3), for Bell's (2013) article "George Wallace Stood in a Doorway at the University of Alabama 50 Years Ago Today" was completed independently during Activity 2. Secondary students independently completed this QAR graphic organizer (i.e., Figure 2.4) during Activity 2 for three files (1) *Why Are Schools Still So Segregated?* (Above the Noise, 2018), (2) *Nearly Six Decades Later, Integration Remains a Work in Progress* (National Public Radio, 2014), and (3) *How the Boston Busing Decision Still Affects City Schools 40 Years Later* (WBUR News, 2014).

- Lesson objective 3: To evaluate students' use of print and technological resources to conduct and present research, a teacher-created rubric should be utilized. Prior to creating the rubric, consider the traits of a successful presentation. Middle school teachers will need to create a rubric for students' small group presentations on the impact of school segregation and desegregation within a local community (i.e., Activity 3). The *Oral Presentation Rubric*, listed in the Additional Online Resources section below, may be of use in creating or adapting a rubric to evaluate the presentations. Secondary teachers will need to create a rubric to evaluate the in-class debate on whether contemporary schools are desegregated yet not integrated or integrated. This rubric will be needed to evaluate learning during Activity 3. The *Debate Rubric*, listed in the Additional Online Resources section below, may be of use to create or adapt a means of evaluating the in-class debate.
- Lesson objective 4: To evaluate students' understanding of and respect for racial and/or ethnic diversity, teachers can utilize the *Teaching Tolerance Anti-Bias Framework*, which is listed in the Additional Online Resources section below. The framework presents grade-level outcomes for students in the following grade bands: K–2, 3–5, 6–8, and 9–12.

CONCLUDING REMARKS

Teachers may utilize *Separate Is Never Equal* and the lessons presented within this chapter to foster discussions of societal issues such as racism, colorism, prejudice, and racially and/or ethnically based discrimination within their classrooms. While this chapter presented lessons primarily for the English language arts and reading classroom, these lessons could easily address curriculum standards set forth by the National Council for the Social Studies.

In fact, the Question-Answer Relationships strategy presented in this chapter is appropriate for the social studies classroom (Ouzts, 1998), and uniform strategy usage is recommended across the content areas (Biancarosa & Snow, 2006). Nevertheless, the use of multicultural children's literature across the content areas is imperative. Multicultural children's literature helps to foster cultural understanding by integrating culturally relevant pedagogy in the content areas.

The lessons presented in this chapter, for example, rely on a transformative approach to culturally relevant pedagogy (Vacca, Vacca, & Mraz, 2017). This transformative approach required students to think critically to generate their own conclusions about historical and contemporary issues surrounding school segregation, desegregation, and resegregation through reading and synthesizing information from various sources.

Moreover, multicultural children's literature such as *Separate Is Never Equal* can be used to affirm and celebrate the accomplishments of students of color, linguistically diverse students, and students of diverse cultural heritage. This is not only important for traditionally marginalized students but also to foster cultural understanding among students from dominant populations.

ADDITIONAL ONLINE RESOURCES

- IRA/NCTE. (2003). *Oral presentation rubric*. Retrieved from www. readwritethink.org/files/resources/printouts/30700_rubric.pdf
- IRA/NCTE. (2005). *Debate rubric*. Retrieved from www.readwrite-think.org/files/resources/lesson_images/lesson819/rubric2.pdf
- Teaching Channel. (2013). *Designing rubrics* [video]. Retrieved from www.teachingchannel.org/video/designing-rubrics
- Teaching Tolerance. (2014). *Teaching Tolerance anti-bias framework*. Montgomery, AL: Southern Poverty Law Center. Retrieved from www. tolerance.org/sites/default/files/general/TT%20anti%20bias%20frame-work%20pamphlet_final.pdf
- Tonatiuh, D. (2014). *Separate is never equal: Sylvia Mendez and her family's fight for desegregation* [audiobook]. Sananes, A. [narrator]. Dreamscape Media. Available at www.amazon.com/Separate-Never-Equal-Duncan-Tonatiuh/dp/1629238562

REFERENCES

Above the Noise. (2018, February 7). *Why are schools still segregated?* Retrieved from www.youtube.com/watch?v=v2TG9n0vc-4&feature=youtu.be

Administrative Office of the U.S. Courts. (2018). *Script—Mendez v. Westminster re-enactment*. Retrieved from www.uscourts.gov/educational-resources/educational-activities/script-mendez-v-westminster-re-enactment

Bell, D. (2013, June 11). George Wallace stood in a doorway at the University of Alabama 50 years ago today. *U.S. News & World Report*. Retrieved from www.us news.com/news/blogs/press-past/2013/06/11/george-wallace-stood-in-a-doorway-at-the-university-of-alabama-50-years-ago-today

Biancarosa, C., & Snow, C. E. (2006). *Reading next—A vision for action and re-search in middle and high school literacy: A report to Carnegie Corporation of New York* (2nd ed.). Washington, DC: Alliance for Excellent Education.

Fenty, N. S., McDuffie-Landrum, K., & Fisher, G. (2012). Using collaboration, co-teaching, and question answer relationships to enhance content area literacy. *Teaching Exceptional Children, 44*(6), 28–37.

Green, S. (2016). Two for one: Using QAR to increase reading comprehension and improve test scores. *The Reading Teacher, 70*(1), 103–109. doi:10.1002/trtr.1466.

International Reading Association and National Council of Teachers of English. (1996). *Standards for the English language arts*. Urbana, IL: International Reading Association and National Council of Teachers of English.

Keith, V. M., & Monroe, C. R. (2016). Histories of colorism and implications for education. *Theory into Practice, 55*(4), 4–10.

Kinniburgh, L. H., & Baxter, A. (2012). Using question answer relationships in science instruction to increase the reading achievement of struggling readers and students with reading disabilities. *Current Issues in Education, 15*(2), 1–9.

Kozak, S., & Recchia, H. (2018). Reading and the development of social understanding: Implications for the literacy classroom. *The Reading Teacher, 72*(5), 1–9. doi:10.1002/trtr.1760.

Levine, P., & Wagner, M. (2003). Secondary school students' experiences in special education classrooms. In M. Wagner, L. Newman, R. Cameto, P. Levine, & C. Marder (Eds.), *Going to school: Instructional contexts, programs, and participation of secondary school students with disabilities. A report from the National Longitudinal Transition Study-2* (pp. 69–76). Menlo Park, CA: SRI International.

May, L. A. (2010). Situating strategies: An examination of comprehension strategy instruction in one upper elementary classroom oriented toward culturally relevant teaching. *Literacy Research and Instruction, 50*(1), 31–43. doi.org/10.1080/19388070903441132.

McIntosh, M. E., & Draper, R. J. (1995). Applying the question-answer relationship strategy in mathematics. *Journal of Adolescent & Adult Literacy, 39*(2), 120–131.

National Council for the Social Studies. (n.d.). *National curriculum standards for social studies: Chapter 2—The themes of social studies*. Retrieved from www.socialstudies.org/standards/strands

National Public Radio, Inc. (2003, June 11). *Wallace in the schoolhouse door*. Retrieved from listenwise.com/teach/lessons/286-george-wallace-at-the-school-door

National Public Radio, Inc. (2014, January 13). *Nearly six decades later, integration remains a work in progress*. Retrieved from listenwise.com/teach/events/159-racial-integration-in-little-rock-decades-later

Ouzts, D. T. (1998). Enhancing the connection between literature and the social studies using the question-answer relationship. *Social Studies and the Young Learner, 10*(4), 26–28.

Raphael, T. E. (1986). Teaching question answer relationships, revisited. *The Reading Teacher, 39*(6), 516–522.

Raphael, T. E., & Au, K. H. (2005). QAR: Enhancing comprehension and test taking across grades and content areas. *The Reading Teacher, 59*(3), 206–221. doi:10.1598/RT.59.3.1.

Scholastic Inc. (2018). *Ruby Bridges and the Civil Rights Movement slide show for grades K–2*. Retrieved from www.scholastic.com/teachers/slideshows/teaching-content/ruby-bridges-and-the-civil-rights-movement-slide-show-for-kinder/

Scholastic Inc. (2018). *Ruby Bridges and the Civil Rights Movement slide show teaching guide, kindergarten to grade 2*. Retrieved from www.scholastic.com/

teachers/articles/teaching-content/ruby-bridges-and-civil-rights-movement-slide-show-teaching-guide-kindergarten-grade-2/#tech-tips
Tonatiuh, D. (2014). *Separate is never equal: Sylvia Mendez and her family's fight for desegregation.* New York: Abrams Books for Young Readers.
Vacca, R. T., Vacca, J. A. L., & Mraz, M. (2017). *Content area reading: Literacy and learning across the curriculum* (12th ed.). Indianapolis, IN: Pearson Education, Inc.
WBUR News. (2014, June 20). *How the Boston busing decision still affects city schools 40 years later.* Retrieved from www.wbur.org/news/2014/06/20/boston-busing-ruling-anniversary

3

Inside Out & Back Again

Making Cultural Connections through Immigrant Food for Early, Middle, and Secondary Learners

Janet K. Keeler

This chapter guides K–12 teachers in ways to use food themes in substantive lessons to connect Thanhha Lai's *Inside Out & Back Again* with their students' own experiences. Though the book is not technically about food, the author uses it to show the characters' connections with their own culture and also the ways in which food creates comfort or causes alienation. The desire for food and the human necessity for nourishment are universal. However, food is an underutilized classroom tool to foster understanding and build cultural competence.

Inside Out & Back Again is the story of a South Vietnamese family that flee their homeland at the end of the Vietnam War in the mid-1970s to escape communism. There are many complicated themes highlighted in the book including immigration and displacement, family, war, global politics, bullying, perseverance, and cultural identity that can be explored in age-appropriate ways.

BACKGROUND OF THE LITERATURE

The young adult novel *Inside Out & Back Again* by Thanhha Lai is a fictionalized account of her family's flight from Saigon in 1975 as South Vietnam fell into the hands of the communists and continues to their eventual resettlement in Alabama. The story is told in easily accessible free verse from the point of view of eleven-year-old protagonist Hà, from her last *Tết* (new year) celebration in Vietnam to life in the American South later that year. The second half of the book focuses on Hà's trials and triumphs in her new home.

The book touches on many themes, including immigration and displacement, family, war, global politics, bullying, perseverance, and cultural identity. While the themes are complicated, Lai's evocative verse written in a child's voice draws attention to universal human experiences. This effective technique elicits compassion and understanding from readers of different cultures and a variety of ages because of the universal themes. The author includes a note to readers in which she reveals her personal connection to the story. In addition there is a Q&A interview with the author, tips for interviewing family and writing poetry, and discussion questions.

Food is mentioned on 42 pages of Lai's 260-page book. It is often the focal point for Hà. At the start of the story, with rumblings of the end of the war in the background, she celebrates one last *Tết* in Saigon with sugar lotus seeds and glutinous rice cakes (Lai, 2011). When her family settles in Alabama, she eats chicken from a "paper bucket" (Lai, 2011, p. 119) for the first time. In between are dreams of her beloved papaya tree that grew in the family's garden and a homage to *nước mắm*, the stinky, fermented fish sauce integral to Southeast Asian cuisine (Lai, 2011).

The lessons in this chapter will show teachers how to use the book's food themes to teach culture in a social studies context. Resources are provided to bolster teachers' understanding of the Vietnam War and the plight of refugees.

PEDAGOGICAL APPROACH

This chapter aims to broaden teachers' cultural awareness of their students and show them how to use nonconfrontational food themes to foster inclusive and sometimes difficult conversations. Students will come to understand how the food and cuisines that immigrants and refugees bring with them enrich American society, and the broader impact is deepening empathy for and acceptance of classmates from different backgrounds.

Immigrant students and first-generation American students may take pride in being recognized and their cultures being celebrated. Using inquiry-circle-based lessons, teachers will guide students through *Inside Out & Back Again*, encouraging them to relate the text to their own lives, thus teaching tolerance and understanding that it will be useful over a lifetime.

This is what Bruner (1960) describes as spiral curriculum. Bruner encourages curriculum developers to consider whether classroom lessons have the potential of making a student a better adult (Bruner, 1960). "A curriculum ought to be built around the great issues, principles, and values that a society deems worthy of the continual concern of its members" (Bruner, 1960, p. 52).

Lessons that cultivate cultural understanding fit that edict. Using spiral curriculum remains pertinent today, but it requires teacher dedication to the material. Coehlo & Moles (2016) write that it only works if the material truly spirals. By that they mean that the information must continue to build and expand rather than just be rehashed year after year, or even week after week. Done right it "activates prior knowledge, initiates interest, and reinforces learning" (Coehlo & Moles, 2016, p. 162).

Cooper (2012–2013) writes that the potential to use food as a teaching tool is untapped as a pathway to cultural understanding. Psilaki (2012) writes that the incorporation of food into the curriculum shows the complexity of human behavior and experience. She uses bread, prepared in many manifestations, as a way for students to taste the food of the "other." Eating the food of the "other" though has in some cases become a crutch or a way for educators to check off the multicultural box on curriculum requirements.

Alenuma-Nimoh (2016) uses the phrase "eating the other multiculturalism" as a way to describe teachers' penchants for teaching diversity by celebrating festivals, "eating exotic foreign food and wearing festival traditional clothing" (p. 128). Mainstream curriculum, largely developed by members of the white dominant culture, is predisposed to this fallback position. "Critical multiculturalism offers a framework that recognizes all the ways in which we are connected by local and global issues that intersect" (2016, p. 128).

To connect with the book and then to their students, teachers themselves should first imagine what it would be like to be an eleven-year-old girl forced to flee her country because the political winds have shifted. Where the family will settle is unknown, but it will surely be better than what home will become. Now they should think about packing the bag that the child will carry on the run, first by foot and then by ship and then by who knows what else. The small bag is stuffed with clothes (not many), shoes, and soap, and Mother says bring "ten palms of rice grains, three clumps of cooked rice" (Lai, 2011, p. 55).

Once teachers fully understand the implications of these simple instructions that precede the young girl's journey into the unknown, they will be able to embrace the curriculum outlined in this chapter. After all, posits Bruner, a curriculum is for teachers before students. "If it cannot change, move, perturb, inform teachers, it will have no effect on those whom they teach" (Bruner, 1960, p. xv).

Though Bruner's thinking is foundational in education curriculum pedagogy, teachers don't always have the foundational knowledge to fully understand and utilize multicultural children's literature effectively. Iwai (2013) writes that many teachers do not understand the importance of diversity and often don't do enough self-evaluation about their biases. This is partly because they have not had enough training.

Bridging the cultural divide can help reduce the achievement gap, which persists despite many efforts to narrow and explain it, including controversial assertions that genetics and natural ability are at play. However, current thinking considers more subtle factors to explain the achievement gap, including negative stereotyping and peer pressure (Ansell, 2011). "Research also has shown that students from a disadvantaged group can perform below their normal ability when confronted with negative stereotypes about their group" (Ansell, 2011, para. 10).

The United States is more racially and culturally diverse than ever, but the primary and secondary teacher workforce remains overwhelmingly middle-class, white, and female. In 2016, 82% of teachers were white (U.S. Department of Education, 2016). Roy (2018) argued that the prevalence of white teachers may lead to predominantly Eurocentric materials being used in the classroom to the exclusion of materials presenting the perspective(s) of people of color. This can be isolating to students of color. Thus, according to Roy (2018), it is imperative that white teachers are intentional about the usage of materials, such as books, centered on people of color.

By 2024, it is expected that the student population will be 56% non-white but current trends show that the nationwide retention figures for African American and Hispanic teachers are lower than for white teachers (U.S. Department of Education, 2016). This does not bode well for diversifying the teacher workforce to mirror student demographics. "Despite the critical role that teachers of color can play in helping students of color succeed, every state has a higher percentage of students of color than teachers of color" (U.S. Department of Education, 2016, p. 9).

Enter the idea of using food to teach culture and Llewellyn's (2002) inquiry circle model as a way to develop critical thinking skills. The stages are questioning, elicitation of existing knowledge, prediction, planning and implementation of the application, commenting, and presenting outcomes. Different age groups can come at Llewellyn's model in different ways, and the activities in this chapter will show teachers of all grades how to do this in lesson ideas with accompanying resources for them.

Take, for example, a fourth-grade class and the examination of bread. That the students eat bread is likely true. Who prepared and/or bought the bread? Study the origin of five types of bread (white, whole wheat, pita, challah, and biscuits, for example). What nourishment do people get from bread? Are all people affected in the same way (allergies!)? How is bread made and where in the store can it be bought? How is bread eaten differently around the world? These questions themselves should spark lesson ideas for teachers.

The making of a sandwich could be a culminating project, or maybe a taste test of different types of bread. (Peanut butter and jelly would be easiest, but allergies must be taken into consideration.)

Food "seems to 'break the ice,' encouraging participation from even the most reticent students since everyone can be considered an authority on their own foodways" (Long, 2010, p. 254). Foodways is the term used to describe the intersection of food with tradition, culture, and history. Food-centric curriculum can be productive and dynamic in social studies (Cooper, 2012–2013). The study of food reveals to students how much we are alike. *You and I Eat the Same*, a collection of essays edited by Chris Ying, underscores this notion as the collection of works takes readers on a global literary tour of the ways in which food unites us.

The desire for food and the human necessity for nourishment are universal. How the food comes to our plates is where the difference resides. Politics, culture, economics, and geography come into play. Hsu (2016) notes that many minority groups gain acceptance and their integration is facilitated through popularization of the food that comes from their countries.

The idea of using food in the classroom is not new but has been done in such a superficial way that it can be viewed as gimmicky (Cooper, 2012–2013). For example, eating tacos on Cinco de Mayo to celebrate Mexican culture has little educational value unless that activity accompanies a discussion about the origins of the food, the human toll of bringing it to our tables, and why Cinco de Mayo is more celebrated in the United States than in Mexico (Cabrero & Lucero, 2018). One area of concern for this curriculum is the sensitivity of teachers when the demographics of the students are different than their own.

For white teachers, racism has been historically difficult to address as teachers often respond with "guilt, silence, denial, or anger" (Irvine, 2003, p. 78). Some strive to be color-blind, treating all students the same, but the unintended consequence is that they are unable or unwilling to see that the level playing field they think they have created is based on their own experiences and paradigms. Feagin (2001) asserts that color-blind ideology is "sincere fiction"; even though at its core is "notions of fairness and nondiscrimination," it "ignores the realities of racism" (p. 110).

The lessons derived from *Inside Out & Back Again* are culturally relevant to the increasingly diverse U.S. student population. While the author focuses on the experiences of a Vietnamese family, the themes of immigration, bullying, acceptance, family, and traditions are pervasive in a diverse society. Using food as a springboard to explore these themes makes them less fraught for teachers still exploring their own beliefs.

The democratic themes of food—humans need it to survive and have strong psychological and emotional connections to it—can be used by teachers to celebrate cultural diversity across disciplines but especially in social studies. With thoughtful and sensitive curriculum planning, multicultural literature such as *Inside Out & Back Again* can help to connect 4–12 teachers and their students with culture in transformative ways.

Lesson Objectives

Based on objectives of the National Council for Social Studies (Loop, n.d.) and National Curriculum Standards for Social Studies (2017), these lessons will:

- Help students to think critically about culture, and encourage them to understand how culture evolves over time and through geopolitical changes. (Culture, Standard 1, and Time, Continuity, and Change, Standard 2)
- Show students how food tells a human story as it intersects with tradition, culture, and history. (People, Places, and Environment, Standard 3, and Power, Authority, and Governance, Standard 6)
- Generate age-appropriate understanding of geography and the globe, using the migration of food as way to illustrate economic and political impact. (Time, Continuity, and Change, Standard 2, and Individual Development and Identity, Standard 4)
- Foster understanding and appreciation for people of diverse backgrounds while discovering and celebrating their own cultures. (People, Places, and Environment, Standard 3)

Content Overview

In these lessons, students from fourth through twelfth grades will learn the impact of food on the development of culture through the lens of a refugee family. A variety of activities, including writing, traditional and multimedia presentations, group discussions, and independent and group research, use Thanhha Lai's *Inside Out & Back Again* as a guide. Through the evocative free verse of the author, teachers can help students draw the cultural connections between the characters in the book, their own lives, and those of their classmates and communities.

Each activity uses a food theme to demonstrate our commonality and thus fosters cultural competence. Food is a universal necessity always accompanied by a personal narrative, which could either be positive or negative. One benefit of these lessons is that teachers can use readily available materials, including many found on the Internet. Teachers will find that food is a good springboard for difficult conversations and also a way to teach empathy and learn about other cultures, especially those of classmates and communities.

For many high school students and teachers, their only exposure to Vietnamese culture may be the Vietnamese dish *phở*, a brothy noodle dish that has become popular in the United States as Vietnamese restaurants have proliferated. A familiar food might be the *bành mí* sandwich of meat, herbs, and pickled vegetables stuffed into a sliced French baguette. French bread made its way to Vietnam in the mid-nineteenth century when France colonized the country. The *bành mí* eventually became a popular street food in Saigon. For teachers, the trail of food is a way to tell stories of people and culture, and these lessons will accomplish that.

For all levels, but especially early learners, a discussion of the book's title, *Inside Out & Back Again*, would be instructive. English language learners specifically would benefit from this because colloquialisms can be difficult concepts. Use a sweater as a visual aid to discuss the concept of "inside out." There is the right way, what we are used to, and the wrong way, the other side or the wrong side.

Sometimes, teachers should tell students, when situations are challenging or uncomfortable, we can feel "inside out." The protagonist of the story felt like that. But then eventually Hà got on firmer footing, so she went from the right side of the sweater, to the wrong side, and then back to the right side.

Materials/Supplies

- Lai, Thanhha. *Inside Out & Back Again*. New York: HarperCollins Children's Books, 2011.
- Computers or devices with Internet access
- World maps and globes
- Library books and encyclopedias
- Audio/visual equipment to share projects with class
- Recording devices, possibly smartphones, for interviews, secondary lessons
- Cameras, possibly smartphones, for interviews, secondary lessons
- Food brought to class
- Poster board, markers, scissors, and glue
- Paper and writing utensils
- Printer

SEQUENCE OF ACTIVITIES

Elementary, Fourth and Fifth Grade

Hook

Discuss as a class the importance of food to all people as a way to nourish their bodies and to celebrate who they are and their backgrounds. Include in the conversation how the food we eat in the United States has roots in other places. (Tomatoes originated in South America, and watermelon is rooted in West Africa.)

Teachers should begin the lesson by having students read the book in class and jot down specific words or historical events that they don't know or understand. These should be explained. Discussion will follow about how some people (refugees) are forced to leave their homes for safer places in other countries. Often, they bring with them food or their memories of it. These lessons will build on that base.

Activity No. 1: Introduction to the Papaya

Depending on the reading levels of the students, the teacher should read out loud or have students read independently or with partners the passages (or a selection of them chosen by the teacher) of the book that mention the protagonist's favorite food, the papaya (pp. 2, 7, 8, 21, 60, 176, 195, 201, 234). What is a papaya? Where does it grow, and more importantly, how does it taste and how is it prepared? Photos of papaya trees plus pictures of the whole and cut fruit can be easily found on the Internet and printed to share with students.

Better yet, teachers should bring a whole papaya, a halved papaya, and chunks of the fruit into the classroom. Students can see and touch the whole papaya and then inspect the shiny seeds described in the book as looking like fish eyes. Do they look like this? Now for a taste. Ask the students to talk about food that brings them comfort, explaining what that means.

Because the papaya is eaten in equatorial countries around the world, this would be a good opportunity to talk about how the word *papaya* is spelled and pronounced in other languages. This could be an inclusive activity for English language learners because it provides an opportunity for them to share their language if they come from a culture where papaya is eaten.

The students will write a sentence about the taste and look of the fruit with the teacher guiding them to use dynamic words. They will also write several sentences about what they learned about the papaya and a few more about what food in their own lives holds special meaning for them.

Resources:

- World map or globe to show where papayas are grown.
- Papaya entry on the World's Healthiest Foods website. Retrieved from www.whfoods.com/genpage.php?tname=foodspice&dbid=47
- "A Map of Where Your Food Originated May Surprise You," from the Salt on NPR. Retrieved from www.npr.org/sections/thesalt/2016/06/13/481586649/a-map-of-where-your-food-originated-may-surprise-you
- "How to Say Papaya in Different Languages." Retrieved from www.indifferentlanguages.com/words/papaya

Activity No. 2: A Poem about Food

In the book, Lai writes in emotional terms about food experiences. As in Activity No. 1, the teacher or several students taking turns should read "American Chicken" on page 119. Reading it out loud will focus the class on the poem. This poem illustrates how the food in the family's new Alabama home is unlike what they ate in Vietnam (vegetables and fruit from their garden compared to chicken from a "paper bucket" or a "white meat" sandwich, which is turkey).

Before they begin writing their poems, put them in pairs or groups of three to talk about the experience. Instruct them to encourage their classmates to try to remember as much as they can about their food memory. Besides the type of food and how it tasted, they should think about where they were and who gave them the food. Can they re-create the experience in words? Poetry is a good vehicle for struggling learners to practice comprehension skills because they have fewer words on which to focus.

It is easy to get lost in long sentences and paragraphs, so verse can help lessen the feeling of being overwhelmed. This is also an opportunity for English language learners to study text in small bits that may make the task of reading less intimidating. Students will write a poem in whatever style they want about the first time they ate a certain food.

Resources:

- "*Out of Wonder* Aims to Inspire a New Generation of Poets," an interview and article with poet Kwame Alexander on NPR. Retrieved from www.npr.org/2017/03/17/520421503/out-of-wonder-aims-to-inspire-a-new-generation-of-poets
- "Meet the Author: Kwame Alexander" from Fairfax Network. Longer interview but includes Q&A with students. Good foundational information for teacher who may find shorter segments to show students. Retrieved from www.youtube.com/watch?v=V39o0u6Wjbg

- "150 Words to Describe the Taste of Food" on Hybrid Rasta Mama. Retrieved from hybridrastamama.com/150-words-to-describe-the-taste-of-food-to-children-and-adults-alike/

Activity No. 3: New Year Food Traditions

Inside Out & Back Again tracks the lives of Hà's family from the Vietnamese celebration of *Tết* (the new year) in 1975 (the Year of the Cat) to *Tết* the following year. In 1975, the New Year was celebrated on Feb. 11, and in 1976 (the Year of the Dragon), it was Jan. 31. Like many Asians, Vietnamese follow the Lunar Calendar for their New Year celebrations. What is the Lunar Calendar and what calendar is used in the West? (The Gregorian Calendar.) The teacher leads a discussion on why different cultures celebrate the New Year at different times and with special food traditions. Around the world, many cultures eat foods to bring them good luck for the new year. In Vietnam, that includes lotus seeds (which represent fertility) and simple sticky rice cakes (representing humbleness and resourcefulness).

For struggling learners, working with another student to study one good luck food focuses them on one concept. This gives them the opportunity to break down the larger concept (global new year's traditions) to one concept (why black-eyed peas are good luck food). Introducing one concept to learners who have memory problems gives them a better chance at success.

Students will work in pairs or groups of three to research one new year's good luck food associated with Asian or American cultures. The teacher should assign a food to each group. The groups will create a poster board of their findings and present it to the class.

Resources:

- YouTube video "Lunar New Year Feast with Helen's Recipes: Tết in Danang." Retrieved from www.youtube.com/watch?v=GnfkN32uthI
- Jeffrey, Laura S. (2008). *Celebrate Tết*. Berkeley Heights, NJ: Enslow Publishers.
- Malaspina, Ann, & Chavarri, Elisa. (2013). *New Year Traditions Around the World*. Mankato, MN: The Child's World.
- "40 Good Luck Foods to Eat on New Year's Day" from *Good Housekeeping*. Retrieved from www.goodhousekeeping.com/holidays/g1960/good-luck-foods/

Additional Resource for Teachers:

- YouTube video, "4 Things to Know Before You Read Thanhha Lai's *Inside Out & Back Again*" on Conley's Cool ESL. Retrieved from www.youtube.com/watch?v=8bWRjajx-LE

Middle

Hook

Students should read the book individually as homework before class discussions and activities begin. Discuss as a class the general concepts of immigration, including the reasons why people leave their native countries, the definition of a refugee, and the notion of assimilation. The challenges and influences of the immigrant experience will be a prominent part of discussions. Food themes will be used to elucidate concepts. For English language learners, this might seem an overwhelming task. Teachers could assign them verses that they feel would best suit their abilities.

Activity No. 1: A Celebration of Immigrant Food

America has often been called a melting pot, but that indicates we've all seamlessly coalesced. At the heart of this lesson is a discussion on whether or not that is true. And do we even want to meld together at the risk of losing culture? Students will brainstorm other food words or phrases to describe America's makeup. Is it more like a salad with lots of distinctive ingredients or a pizza with a common foundation and a variety of toppings (opinions and tastes)?

What immigrant cuisines (Chinese, Vietnamese, French, Greek, Moroccan, Mexican, Italian, Cuban, Thai, Jamaican, etc.) are served in restaurants within a few miles of where they live? Food for thought: Does all this seem like American food now? And is there a true American cuisine?

Students will use computers to access maps and businesses to find the restaurants within a few miles of their homes. They will create a list of the restaurant names and also what types of cuisines are served there. (If they don't know, they can call and ask.) In a class discussion, the students will share what they found and the teacher will tally the different cuisines.

Resources:

- "Foodways" from Immigration to the United States. Retrieved from immigrationtounitedstates.org/504-foodways.html
- Gabaccia, Donna. (2000). *We Are What We Eat: Ethnic Food and the Making of Americans*. Cambridge, MA: Harvard University Press.

Activity No. 2: How Does It Feel to Be Hungry?

Hà, her brothers, and her mother are fleeing Saigon on a ship, but they do not know where they are going or for how long they will be traveling. They are unsure of what food will be available, and there are many verses in the book that address what they ate (or what they longed for) on the journey. Besides some clothes and a personal item called "one choice" in the book, they can bring ten palmsful of uncooked rice grains and three clumps of cooked rice.

Teachers should bring to class a large container of uncooked rice and have each student fill one palm with the grains and then measure the amount. Have students do the math: 10 times their palmful (likely about 1/4 of a cup to start) and then double that because rice expands that much in cooking. So if they initially get 2.5 cups, they'll have five cups cooked. Bring in a bowl of cooked rice to show how much that is.

How long do the students think it will be before they run out of food? Discuss the topic of food insecurity, which exists in many cities, large and small, in the United States. Food-insecure people don't know where their next meal is coming from. Teachers are likely to have students in their classes who are food insecure and hungry so the idea of not having enough to eat cuts across cultures and situations. Tread lightly and do not force a group discussion about hunger or risk alienating or "otherizing" students.

Teachers who select this activity should understand the basic properties of cooking rice and should also be informed about the topic of food insecurity and hunger in the United States. The resources below should help teachers gain more understanding about these issues.

Before the activity, students will write an essay about what hunger means to them. After the activity, students will be asked to read their essay again and write a paragraph about their reaction to what they wrote. Would they change anything?

Resources:

- Guest speaker. Invite a representative from a local food bank to visit the class to talk about hunger issues in the community and what is being done to alleviate/combat them.
- "Ester Ndichu: Hunger Isn't a Food Issue. It's a Logistics Issue." (2015). Ted Talk video. Retrieved from https://www.youtube.com/watch?v=oXlMn3WGHkE
- No Kid Hungry, a report of hunger in American schools. Retrieved from www.nokidhungry.org/sites/default/files/HIOS.pdf

Activity No. 3: Nearly Every Culture Eats Rice

While rice is integral to Vietnamese cuisine, it is also a staple in the diet of other Asian countries and many more places around the world. Imagine Latin American food without arroz con pollo or Italian offerings without risotto.

Rice is central to many African dishes. Every Greek diner serves rice pudding. How and where is rice grown and what are its origins?

It is likely most students will not have seen a rice paddy or even know that rice is grown in fields flooded with water. Show the twenty-two-minute documentary *One Day in the Life of a Rice Farmer* about a Filipino farmer and show them photos from the Internet. Have the students talk about their impressions of the documentary. Then explain the group activity, put them in groups, and give each group a country to research. For example, some Vietnamese say that the country looks like a rice basket hanging from two ends of a pole. In many countries, rice is used as an offering to deities. Throwing rice at newlyweds as they leave the ceremony is meant to represent fertility. What else does rice symbolize?

Students will conduct a group research project on how different cultures use rice in cooking and what special attributes they consider rice to have both nutritionally and culturally. The groups will present their findings to the class.

Resources:

- *One Day in the Life of a Rice Farmer*. Retrieved from https://topdocumentaryfilms.com/one-day-life-rice-farmer/

Additional Resources for Teachers:

- Ricepedia.com
- MacDonald, Fiona, & Faleschini, Gian Paolo. (2001). *Discovering World Cultures: Food*. New York: Crabtree.
- California Rice Commission. calrice.org

Secondary

Hook

Students should read the book individually as homework before class discussion and activities begin. Discuss as a class the general concepts of immigration, including refugees, bullying, and the Vietnam War, using food themes as a jumping-off point for discussion. Students will also come to learn how other cultures and cuisine from around the world have become part of the fabric of America.

Activity No. 1: What Is a Refugee?

The Vietnam War might as well be ancient history to many students in high school today. Perhaps they have a grandparent who served, on either side of the conflict, but their connection to the war is likely tenuous. For many young people of non–Southeast Asian descent, their sole association with Vietnamese people might be the workers at their favorite walk-in nail salon. (There is a good discussion there about how Asian nail salons came to proliferate in the United States.)

Because so much of *Inside Out & Back Again* addresses the flight from Vietnam, there is an opportunity to use photojournalism to show how that looked. A simple Internet search of "fall of Saigon photos" and "fall of Saigon food" will turn up iconic Associated Press images of the chaotic last days of a democratic South Vietnam. The food photos show refugees fleeing with arms cradling boxes and containers of food. Also readily available are photos of refugees working their way through food lines at camps. Have students study these photos and draw the connection through discussion between Hà's descriptions of what they ate and how that was even a consideration as they fled. For both struggling learners and English language learners, the visual cues of the photographs can help connect them to the book's messages in ways that the words may not.

Put students in groups and have them discuss their feelings about the images they study using one or two words. Ask one student in each group to record the words. Each student will take the list of words and write a poem from them.

Resources:

- World map to study the cities of Vietnam, north and south
- "Fall of Saigon Through the Eyes of AP Photographers." NamViet News. Retrieved from namvietnews.wordpress.com/40th-anniversary-of-the-fall-of-saigon/fall-of-saigon-through-the-eyes-of-ap-photographers/
- "Lessons of the Fall of Saigon." *Time Magazine.* Retrieved from time.com/3840657/saigon-fall-lessons/
- "Saigon: The Final Hours." (2015). Fifteen-minute documentary from WBUR on fortieth anniversary. Retrieved from www.youtube.com/watch?v=LA3uVYXZAk
- "Home." Poem by Warsan Shire. Retrieved from genius.com/Warsan-shire-home-annotated

Additional Resources for Teachers:

- "12 Amazing Vietnam War Teaching Resources From PBS." We are Teachers. Retrieved from www.weareteachers.com/vietnam-war-teaching-resources/

- "The Vietnam War—How is it Taught in Vietnam?" Teaching Channel. Retrieved from www.teachingchannel.org/video/teaching-vietnam-war

Activity No. 2: Words Matter

Classmates and townspeople bully Hà and her brothers in Alabama. One of the insults that they throw at her is "pancake face." Read out loud or ask one student to read this poem from the book (pp. 196–197). Lead a discussion to help them imagine being in a new place and being called something that you perceive to be an insult but of which you don't understand the meaning.

She has never heard of a pancake, but it is used to deride the shape of her face. "One foot on a banana peel and the other foot in the grave," "spill the beans," "butter somebody up" and "have your cake and eat it too" are common expressions that are slightly neutral. However, food imagery can also be used in insults such as "couch potato," "full of beans," and "bad egg."

Divide students into groups and have them research a collection of idioms (fish, fruit and vegetables, meat and potatoes, eggs, sweet and sour, etc.) and make a multimedia presentation to the class that includes the origin/history of the phrase.

Resources:

- "Food Idioms: Explanations and Examples." YourDictionary.com. Retrieved from examples.yourdictionary.com/examples-of-food-idioms.html
- "20 Juicy English Expressions that Go Way Beyond Food." FluentU.com. Retrieved from www.fluentu.com/blog/english/english-expressions/
- Foltz, Charlotte. (2018). *Eat Your Words: A Fascinating Look at the Language of Food*. New York: Delacorte Press.

Activity No. 3: Comfort Food in Hard Times

Hà and her family were part of the great migration of Southeast Asian refugees to the United States. Who brought them to the United States and why did they come here? In Hà's case, a man from Alabama agreed to sponsor a refugee family and give them shelter in his home. His wife was not happy about this nor were the neighbors.

Help your students to understand that many Americans had a difficult time accepting the refugees that they felt were their enemies just months before. They did not understand the difference between North and South Vietnam, and the protracted war and high American death toll (58,000 troops) created deep wounds and discord.

In the book, two people stand out as helpers: "the cowboy" who shelters the family and a kind woman who helps Hà to understand the ways of America. Hà is surprised to learn that the woman's son was a U.S. soldier killed in Vietnam. What makes some people want to help others, even when their position may not be popular?

Start the lesson by reading the verses that show how the helpers use food to ease tensions and create comfort, including "Cowboy's Gifts" on page 178 and "MiSSSisss WaSShington's Response" on page 200. Show the Ted Talk video "How a Team of Chefs Fed Puerto Rico after Hurricane Maria."

Students will conduct and record interviews with five family members or important people in their lives about their ideas of comfort food. Encourage them to tell the stories of "why" rather than just list food. Include photographs with the written report.

Resources:

- "How a Team of Chefs Fed Puerto Rico after Hurricane Maria." Chef Jose Andres's twenty-one-minute Ted Talk. Retrieved from www. ted.com/talks/jose_andres_how_a_team_of_chefs_fed_puerto_rico_after_hurricane_maria
- "The Secret to Happiness is Helping Others." Time.com. Retrieved from time.com/collection-post/4070299/secret-to-happiness/

Additional Resources for Teachers:

- "Episode 37: 30 Questions with Lane DeGregory." Twenty-six-minute podcast with a Pulitzer Prize–winning reporter of the *Tampa Bay Times* in St. Petersburg, FL. This episode can help the teacher to guide their students about interviewing subjects using open-ended questions. Retrieved from www.tampabay.com/blogs/writelane/2018/08/29/episode-37-thirty-questions/

CONCLUDING REMARKS

It is likely that some teachers will need to educate themselves on foodways and even the Vietnam War before using these lessons to accompany *Inside Out & Back Again*. It has already been stated but it bears repeating that the term "foodways" is used to describe the intersection of food with tradition, culture, and history. We are all experts in our own foodways, but it might take some coaxing and guidance to bring that out of students and show them the value of this.

Ask students about their first food memories, and they will start with what they ate, maybe ice cream, pizza, or spaghetti. On further prodding, those memories will reveal the who, what, when, where, and why of those foods. The stories of family and comfort, displacement and confrontation may be the final destination of those memories. They will almost never really be about the food or the taste of it, but more likely about feelings and situations.

The food simmering on the pages of *Inside Out & Back Again* is a worthy vehicle for the study of culture, history, and even politics. Thanhha Lai has written a book that can spawn lessons across the curriculum, and certainly ones that can be carried forward in a students' educational career. The study of food is transformative because it allows literature and education to connect with students in a personal way.

REFERENCES

Alenuma-Nimoh, S. J. (2016). Reexamining the concept of multicultural education: Recommendations for moving beyond "eating the other" multiculturalism. *Journal of Intercultural Disciplines, 15*. Retrieved from http://eds.a.ebscohost.com. ezproxy.lib.usf.edu/eds/pdfviewer/pdfviewer?vid=5&sid=8d787dbe-550c-407a-94fe-727e25e5f57f%40sdc-v-sessmgr01

Ansell S. (2011). Achievement gap. *Education Week.* Retrieved from http://www. edweek.org/ew/issues/achievement-gap/

Bruner, J. S. (1960). *The process of education: A landmark in education theory*. Cambridge, MA: Harvard University Press.

Cabrero, C. E., & Lucero, L. (2018, May 5). What is Cinco de Mayo? *New York Times*. Retrieved from https://www.nytimes.com/2018/05/05/business/cinco-de-mayo-facts-history.html

Coelho, C. S., & Moles, D. R. (2016). Student perceptions of a spiral curriculum. *European Journal of Dental Education, 20*(3), 161–166. doi:10.1111/eje.12156.

Cooper, E. E. (2012–2013). Something to sink their teeth into: Teaching culture through food. *Transformations: The Journal of Inclusive Scholarship & Pedagogy*, (2), 92–100.

Feagin, J. (2001). *Racist America: Roots, current realities, and future reparations*. New York: Routledge.

Hsu, M. Y. (2016). On the possibilities of food writing as a bridge between the popular and the political. *Journal of American History, 103*(3), 682–685. doi:10.1093/jahist/jaw330.

Irvine, J. J. (2003). *Educating teachers for diversity: Seeing with a cultural eye*. New York: Teachers College.

Iwai, Y. (2013). Multicultural children's literature and teacher candidates' awareness and attitudes toward cultural diversity. *International Electronic Journal of Elementary Education, 5*(2), 185–198. Retrieved from http://eds.a.ebscohost.com.

ezproxy.lib.usf.edu/eds/pdfviewer/pdfviewer?vid=15&sid=9e2a0f07-233b-4416-84cb-385f369145a8%40sessionmgr4010

Lai, T. (2011). *Inside out & back again.* New York: HarperCollins Children's Books.

Llewellyn, D. (2002). *Inquiry within: Implementing inquiry-based science standards.* Thousand Oaks, CA: Corwin.

Long, L. M. (2010). Nourishing the academic imagination: The use of food in teaching concepts of culture. *Food and Foodways, 9*(3/4).

Loop, Erica. (n.d.). What are the major goals & objectives of social studies education? *Synonym.* Retrieved from https://classroom.synonym.com/major-objectives-social-studies-education-6803269.html

National Curriculum Standards. (2017). Chapter 2: Themes of social studies. Retrieved from https://www.socialstudies.org/standards/strands#1

Psilaki, E. (2012). Sharing culture through food: Teaching in a multicultural university classroom. *The Journal of Inclusive Scholarship and Pedagogy, 23*(2). Retrieved from http://eds.a.ebscohost.com.ezproxy.lib.usf.edu/eds/pdfviewer/pdfviewer?vid=2&sid=8d7 87dbe-550c-407a-94fe-727e25e5f57f%40sdc-v-sessmgr01

Roy, L. A. (2018). *Teaching while white: Addressing the intersections of race and immigration in the classroom.* Lanham, MD: Rowman & Littlefield.

U.S. Department of Education (2016). *The state of educator diversity in the workforce.* Washington, DC: U.S. Department of Education. Retrieved from https://www2.ed.gov/rschstat/eval/highered/racial-diversity/state-racial-diversity-workforce.pdf

Ying, C. (Ed.). (2018). *You and I eat the same: On the countless ways food and cooking connect us to one another.* New York: Artisan.

4

Exploring *Marlon Bundo* as an Artifact for Analysis

Culture Circles and Critical Inquiry toward Informed Civic Engagement

Kevin R. Magill

In this chapter, *A Day in the Life of the Vice President* and *A Day in the Life of Marlon Bundo* serve as a way to discuss/teach children about marriage equality. Through the process, students will be asked to consider the role of literature as a way to promote civil rights and how literary concepts such as satire, hyperbole, caricature, and irony can be used to challenge inequality.

Further, the lesson is designed to help students become more critically literate and discerning civic participants as they conduct social inquiry (research), have difficult discussions, make informed interpretations, and do more socially just forms of social analysis for positive social change. These texts and the skills used to analyze them attempt to align with the National Council for the Social Studies (NCSS) goal of helping students become educated and inspired for lifelong inquiry and informed civic action.

BACKGROUND OF THE LITERATURE

A Day in the Life of the Vice President by Charlotte and Karen Pence is an educational story explaining the job of vice president of the United States to children. The book describes a typical day for Mike Pence as seen through the eyes of the Pence family pet rabbit, Marlon Bundo, which they lovingly refer to as BOTUS or Bunny of the United States.

The story chronicles the experiences of Marlon as he follows the vice president, who the rabbit understands to be his "Grandpa." Marlon visits the Oval Office, the Senate, the vice president's office, and the Naval Observatory. The story ends as Marlon joins the vice president in prayer before bed.

The text is helpful as a factual accounting of vice presidential responsibilities and daily routine.

A Day in the Life of Marlon Bundo is a children's book satirizing *A Day in the Life of the Vice President* and troubles some of the omitted political realities and limited perspectives (authoritarianism, civil rights violations) reflected in the administration of President Trump. It does this by complexifying the story of *A Day in the Life of the Vice President* by giving the vice president's pet rabbit, Marlon Bundo, his own story in which he asserts his agency as a citizen with a homosexual identity.

By emphasizing Marlon Bundo's homosexuality and the agency he and other characters have, the story provides a potentially comforting narrative for those who feel the Trump administration has demonstrated bigoted, alienating, and antiquated relational politics. The rabbit and his friends indirectly critique the public homophobia of Vice President Pence and the authoritarian rhetoric of the Trump administration by providing a narrative where the rabbit has democratic rights, an actual personality apart from the vice president, and his own political mind.

PEDAGOGICAL APPROACH

This chapter proposes to teach students the skills of dialogue, social analysis, and historical inquiry (research). These skills have been shown to be vital to becoming engaged as citizens (Magill, 2018). Generally speaking, inquiry in the social studies is the process by which a social scientist engages in asking for additional information/sources to develop a more complex interpretation of a social, historical, geographic, economic, civic, or physiological event.

This lesson will teach students that choice of artifact or primary source will affect the ultimate narrative (story) a social scientist (or historian) will create. Similarly, the lesson will show that dialogue is vital to helping us better understand how complex social relationships, rules, norms, and policies differently affect people. If the teacher desires, they can also discuss the ways dialogue helps groups form consensus for shared civic action.

This lesson is potentially important because students are often expected to exist as passive citizens where their primary function is to re-create given social structures and relationships. Furthermore, schooling is often set up so it is easy for social studies teachers to accept curriculum as given or others' interpretations as a foundational, necessary, and monolithic part of their subject area.

What is often not taught is that history and social perspectives are interpretive, reflecting the political perspectives of their authors. Textbook curriculum tends to *emphasize* a national story of progress, exceptionalism, and freedom that often excludes marginalized populations. When student stories (or interpretations) are left out, when narratives are incongruent with their understandings of fairness, or when stories they are told do not align with the ways they understand the world, students often reject much of what they learn in these classrooms (Levstik & Barton, 2011; Loewen, 2008; VanSledright, 2008).

A similar problem is that alienated, marginalized, and minoritized historical groups are less recognized in history, but even when they are recognized, their stories are often distilled to fit a model figure whose story aligns with the dominant group's narrative (see, for example, Naseem-Rodriguez, 2018; Vickery, 2017).

Consider here the narratives of Rosa Parks and Martin Luther King Jr., who often represent the whole civil rights movement. Both were trained as activists and labor organizers, yet their narratives portray an old woman sitting on a bus and a man with a dream (Kohl, 1994). The texts and artifacts chosen and used to tell these stories tend to reinforce the social narratives that leave particular social groups invisible and their historical agency limited.

However, dialogue and inquiry are optimistic approaches for helping to illuminate marginalized narratives. Scholarship has shown that student research and interpretive exchange can help students become engaged critical inquirers. With this skill, students can trouble the limited narratives that situate dominant historical understandings, helping them make more complete sense of the power that exists in the world around them (Wineburg, 2001; Salinas & Blevins, 2013).

In the social studies, this process is called *critical* historical inquiry and is based on three main assumptions (Salinas & Blevins, 2013). First, that society is constructed through subjective interpretations based on historical reasoning of primary sources and artifacts (Barton & Levstik, 2004; VanSledright, 2002). Second, that historical interpretation does not occur tabula rasa (as a blank slate). Instead interpretation is a cultural act by which students learn about the nature of the world by playing a role in the historical knowledge creation process (Stearns et al., 2000).

Lastly, the approach "asks that authors reveal their choices and reasoning, consequently making the author's interpretive process central to historical reasoning" (Salinas, Franquiz, & Naseem-Rodriguez, 2016, p. 423; Blankenship & Salinas, 2013; Wineburg, 2001). Opportunities for this type of sociohistorical exploration help students begin "organizing events in a narrative that will show us something important about our position on the world" (Seixas & Peck, 2004, p. 111).

Through inquiry, students expand their own narrative interpretations about the world. Developing a historical narrative allows students to create a schema (pattern of thought or behavior) by which they can understand the social world, engage with another culture, and transform the world in support of a properly functioning democracy. Therefore, in addition to inquiry, students require opportunities for exchanges of their personal interpretations about the world.

The exchange is also vital to democratically understanding the shared and divergent perspectives needed for civic acting. One way to achieve this is through culture circles. Culture circles are a literacy practice that has helped students engage in the process of applying (personal and group) social interpretations to civic praxis (moving theory or ideas to action) (see Freire, 2000).

The process begins with the teacher inviting students to describe themselves, their cultural background, their customs, and their understandings of a given topic. Student ideas can be nuanced/informed by classroom discussions of their personal and cultural relationship to literature, artifacts, and concepts. Students can then develop group consensus as they work to interpret, understand, and transform ideas together (Roberts, 2000). The process involves a "critical praxiological cycle" where students generate themes, problem pose, dialogue, problem solve, and hopefully act (Souto-Manning, 2010).

The group considers the ways textbook-type knowledge can be nuanced by personal and cultural interpretations. Through shared understandings, students can relate their analysis to real-world issues. Teachers and students can repeat the process as they learn more about the topic, about themselves, and about the world. Alternatively, they can discuss more complex issues as they become more aware of the relationship between culture and society.

Lesson Objectives

The NCSS (National Counsel for the Social Studies) mission is to work toward a world in which all students are educated and inspired for lifelong inquiry and informed civic action. The Social Studies C3 framework (College, Career, and Civic Life) suggests students of all ages should be proficient in understanding and applying civic inquiry, understanding interdisciplinary knowledge (particularly as it relates to English language arts), evaluating sources, and communicating their conclusions to take informed actions.

This lesson is based on these foundational ideas and will support student development of these skills by:

- teaching students skills related to social/historical inquiry, critical thinking, social analysis, and intersubjective exchange (discussion);

- teaching to identify difference in historical narrative and interpretation (to change the ways we understand others and society);
- helping students become critically literate and discerning civic participants; and
- furthering interdisciplinary study in examination of satire.

The following lesson can be modified in many ways. Teachers with younger students may want to consider combining Day 1 and Day 2 (removing the more difficult artifacts such as Executive Order 9981 or the Civil Rights Act of 1964 and replacing them with more pictures or civil rights examples they may be familiar with: Rosa Parks, for example) as a way to teach social inquiry (research). Also, teachers may want to substitute sources, artifacts, and topics based on the cultural understandings and experiences of the student population or the political leanings in their region.

Content Overview

In the lesson activities that follow, students will *examine* primary and secondary sources, *conduct an inquiry* into civil rights issues related to marriage equality, discuss ideological differences (differences in our ideas and ideals, especially as they form the basis of economic or political theory and policy), and propose ways to attend to the issue as citizens. Then students will *consider* how satire (and possibly media) can change the nature of a political conversation by comparing the narratives, experiences, and agency in *A Day in the Life of the Vice President* and *A Day in the Life of Marlon Bundo*.

Materials/Supplies

- Pence, C., & Pence, K. (2018). *A day in the life of the vice president.* Washington, DC: Regnery.
- Twiss, J., & Keller, E. G. (2018). *A day in the life of Marlon Bundo.* San Francisco: Chronicle Books.
- Computers or devices with Internet access (or copies of student selected sources)
- Webpages where students can find appropriate sources (e.g., *The New York Times*, National Archives, the Library of Congress, government websites, regional newspapers)
- Historical Thinking Questions about the documents/artifacts developed by the teacher and related to Significance, Epistemology (What do you notice?); Continuity and Change (What is different and what has remained the same in the two sources?); Progress and Decline (What has

improved? What has gotten worse?); Empathy (What did this author think?); and Agency (How were people responsible for bringing about change?)

- (Optional) primary and secondary documents related to civil rights (suggestions are listed in the description below)   .
- Notebooks and paper
- Writing utensils
- (Optional) video clips:
  - Karen & Charlotte Pence: www.youtube.com/watch?v=yUjMIKFQd Rw
  - John Oliver: Marlon Bundo Children's Book: www.youtube.com/watch?v=NsiTCFA_E54
  - Abbreviated version of the above clips: www.youtube.com/watch?v=oB6ex5itrA0

SEQUENCE OF ACTIVITIES

Elementary, Middle, and Secondary

Variability is based on choice of sources or amount of teacher contextualization given.

Day 1. Initial Activity: Review the Inquiry Process

The teacher will contextualize the issue of marriage equality for analyzing the focal books. The teacher may want to consider presenting the concept of social inquiry (the skills of asking for information to create a narrative or schema) prior to the lesson. Teaching inquiry can begin first by having students ask a question about a topic they want to know more about. For example, what are the reasons some people do not want same-sex couples to marry? Why do they feel this way? Have students describe documents, information, or artifacts that they believe can help them answer the inquiry questions they and you propose. Depending on what has been taught previously, you may want to practice dialogue (consider using sentence stems, such as "I believe . . . " or "I noticed . . . " or "I appreciate what [student] said but feel . . . ").

Consider further contextualizing the political battle for marriage equality and the stance of Vice President Pence. For example, consider discussing that the vice president had a radio show where he described religious reasons for his stance on marriage before his current position and that Karen Pence had taught anti-gay ideas to students.

Define satire (the use of humor, irony, exaggeration, or ridicule to expose and criticize people's foolishness or vices, particularly in the context of contemporary politics and other topical issues). To quickly teach satire, also consider introducing examples of hyperbole, caricature, and irony based on a familiar topic. Political cartoons are often helpful examples (example search: "The Screening Process We Wish We Had").

Have a short group discussion about these concepts and record the ideas students share. Ask them where they believe they can find more information (news, documents, personal stories, pictures). Keep these notes visible to the class as a way to begin your inquiry into civil rights and to teach inquiry as research. You may want to help students with their ideas and refer back to things or refine their questions as they learn more about associated issues.

Day 1. Hook

Have students brainstorm the ideas they have about marriage and civil rights. (Perhaps ask students: "What do you think of when you hear marriage and what do you think of when you hear civil rights?") Develop a "T" chart where student answers are written on the whiteboard or on a poster with one concept on each side. Ask students what they know about what civil rights are and how they are achieved. Depending on grade level, ask them to share what they understand about the current social movements related to marriage equality. Do a KWL Chart, which means to ask students what they know (K) and what they would like to know (W) about the issue. Lastly students complete the chart with information they learned (L).

Day 1. Activity No. 1: Developing Historical Narratives

Explain that what historians do when they create a document like a textbook is that they develop a "historical narrative" based on primary sources (an artifact, document, diary, manuscript, autobiography, recording, or any other source of information that was created at the time under study and that serves as an original source of information about the topic). Define "primary source" and quickly discuss historical thinking (described in pre-activity: a set of critical literacy skills for evaluating and analyzing primary source documents to construct a meaningful account of the past). Explain what a "dominant narrative" is (the narrative created to focus our attention on a particular way of looking at an idea) and have a short discussion about the dominant narrative of citizenship (that civic expectations tend to be about voting but that we can do more).

Ask students to consider a textbook example of your (teacher's) choosing. What information would change the way we understand the textbook narrative (ask students to research new sources). Explain that the class will be developing their own narrative (story) after researching more about it.

Day 1. Activity No 2: Marriage Equality

Discuss, in general terms, why marriage equality is a civic right that many have fought for and why it matters. Relate this to the answers that the students gave in the first activity. Divide students into groups and provide them with documents/artifacts and essential/historical thinking questions (related to the following questions: What do you notice? What is different and what has remained the same? What has improved and what is worse? What did the author think? How were people responsible for bringing about change?).

Your questions are designed to help them access information in the sources/artifacts. Further questions could include: How have Americans worked to achieve equal rights under the law? How has marriage been defined? What challenge do same-sex couples face?

Next, provide context for securing equal rights and mention that the class will be researching marriage equality. Offer each group of students two to three primary sources, pictures, and/or some secondary sources (depending on grade level), which could include full (Secondary) or annotated versions (Secondary, Middle, and Elementary). Sources to consider could include:

- Executive Order 9066
- Executive Order 9981
- The Civil Rights Act of 1964
- Speech by Harvey Milk
- *Goodridge v. Department of Public Health*
- Letter from Mayor Gavin Newsome to County Clerk (San Francisco)
- New Hampshire HB 436
- Examples from "Standing Rock"
- Examples from "Occupy Wall Street"
- Examples from "Occupy Alcatraz"

For elementary in particular, teachers may want to consider more pictures and other grade-appropriate narratives related to individuals like Rosa Parks. Secondary sources may be easier for younger students as they might more easily explain these social movements. Ask students to write about the different ways that citizens have worked to achieve marriage equality under the law through civic resistance. Have students take notes and write a short historical narrative (a story combining the information they gathered) about marriage equality and civil rights based on what they discovered in their documents and materials.

Day 1. Activity No. 3: Inquiry

Ask students to ask for new information by researching the questions they still have about the civil rights movement or marriage equality. Ask them to add their new findings (their research) to their narrative and to the KWL chart that was created at the beginning of the lesson. Be sure to suggest the types of documents that are reliable (e.g., the Library of Congress versus a personal webpage with no attribution). Provide some suggested webpages and places to find other sources (some are provided). Students can present the narratives they have created at the teacher's discretion.

Day 2. Hook

Begin by again reminding students how marriage equality is understood politically and the civil rights battles you previously discussed/researched. Next, provide students appropriate grade-level video/audio clips or quotes representing the vice president's (and family's) stance on marriage equality (example: "What Karen Pence's Gay Former Student Wants Her to Know | Opinions | NowThis").

Remind students of the definition of satire and provide students with a related political cartoon where the marriage equality conversation is satirized (example: "Do you remember when being a racist homophobic would've stopped you becoming president?"). Ask students to identify other examples of satire they have seen. Tell students that books can be satire and that today they will examine a piece of satire related to the vice president's stance on marriage equality. Ask students to brainstorm how satire might be used to further civil rights.

Day 2. Activity No. 1: A Day in the Life of the Vice President

Restate that historical or social inquiry requires that we understand how many pieces of evidence fit together. Therefore, we should look at several artifacts to create a narrative related to an issue. Discuss that social studies' purpose is to help us better understand our culture so we can work to make society better for people. Show the video clip (or the abbreviated clip) of Karen and Charlotte Pence discussing their book (provided).

Students conduct a first reading of *A Day in the Life of the Vice President*. Students take notes on what they believe to be the lessons the book is trying to teach and what the writers of this text believe to be important when telling a story (these will likely be the technical aspects of the vice president's day). Next, ask them to describe Bundo based on the text (the book also includes a section in the back that describe some of the duties, routines, and buildings associated with the vice president, which may be of interest).

Day 2. Activity No. 2: Introducing Marlon Bundo

Show clips of "John Oliver: Marlon Bundo Children's Book" (make the decision on which clips to show based on time allotted and the appropriateness of the clips for the particular age group). Have students take basic notes on the clips and on how Oliver is providing satire to promote civic rights.

Day 2. Activity No. 3: A Day in the Life of Marlon Bundo

Have students read *A Day in the Life of Marlon Bundo* and take notes on what they believe to be the lessons the book is trying to teach and what these writers believe is important. Next, ask students to discuss differences in the two Bundos and narratives (stories). Contextualize this by having students consider how the characters might be active or passive or have a personality or not.

Then ask students to consider who the characters in the book represent and how the support they gave to the other animals is a civil rights idea called solidarity. Discuss solidarity in relation to civics (that people organize, protest, and act to change unequal social relationships). Ask students what else they believe the animals could do to help support Marlon Bundo based on the ways they understand civil rights.

Ask students to think about how Marlon Bundo might feel as a homosexual rabbit in the home of someone that does not believe in marriage equality. Then ask students to create a "counter narrative" (a different understanding/ story than the author's description) by adding what they learned from *A Day in the Life of Marlon Bundo* to nuance/change the original description of Bundo.

Day 3. Activity No. 1: Culminating Discussion (optional)

Help students further compare *A Day in the Life of Marlon Bundo* and *A Day in the Life of the Vice President*. Ask students how changing the way they understood Bundo changes the way someone understands citizenship, marriage equality, or civil rights. Ask students why their first description of Bundo is different from the way it looks now. Next, have students brainstorm ways they can support other civil rights causes through art, satire, research, discussion, and action.

Tips for Struggling/Reluctant Readers

Both texts are picture books written for K–4 students. As such, both can be used for struggling or reluctant readers. The texts can be utilized by older students to engage in civic inquiry and analyze complex themes. Teachers will want to consider modifying the inquiry section of the lesson based on grade level, where notes are provided. For example, teachers can use annotated/translated versions of legislation, pictures, video clips of the events, or their descriptions. Additionally, the video clips about the books will provide scaffolds for learning.

Some other ways that this lesson can be differentiated for struggling or reluctant readers may also include, but are not limited to, tiering the assignments based on the student's level of readiness, creating inquiry interest centers/groups to motivate the students, or using flexible grouping or choice boards to select activities from a variety of learning styles.

Tips for English Language Learners

Some ways that this lesson can be differentiated for English language learners include, but are not limited to, providing comprehensible input (miming the actions or showing pictures while discussing), relating the content to the student's background/using inquiry examples based on student background, using/being open to a variety of types of assessment, differentiating the tasks, allowing for collaboration between students, using flexible grouping, and making the content comprehensible for all students through books or charts written in the student's first language or simplified English.

These strategies allow for the English language learners to learn the same concepts as the other students in the classroom while acquiring their English language skills.

Evaluation of Skills

Student skills can be evaluated at every stage of the process. Teachers can collect narratives, note participation in discussions, and assess the sources that students choose. If the teacher desires, they can have students conduct another inquiry into a new topic as a summative assessment of skills.

A teacher may want to fill out the final part of the KWL chart and/or have students develop their own piece of satire. If students decide to take political action based on their culture circle discussions, you may analyze their plans or have them share how their experiences changed their perspectives.

Additional Online Resources

- Potential sources provided by Teaching Tolerance: tinyurl.com/yyogqevy (Executive Order 9066, Executive Order 9981, the Civil Rights Act of 1964, Speech by Harvey Milk, *Goodridge v. Department of Public Health*, letter from Mayor Gavin Newsome to County Clerk [San Francisco], New Hampshire HB 436)
- Potential sources provided by Pro/Con: tinyurl.com/y2qsyf9x (a list is provided on the webpage)
- *The New York Times*: www.nytimes.com/ (example article: "Supreme Court Ruling Makes Same-Sex Marriage a Right Nationwide")
- National Archives: www.archives.gov/ (example: https://historyhub. history.gov/thread/3281)
- The Library of Congress: www.loc.gov/ (example: www.loc.gov/search /?in=&q=civil+rights+activists&new=true)
- Government websites and other regional newspapers (consider your local government):
  ○ tinyurl.com/y5czvrz2
  ○ www.hrc.org/mei/search/texas/waco
- Google Search images of protesters (example: tinyurl.com/y4pvqqje)

Note: Any properly sourced articles that are relevant to a discussion of satire, history, or marriage equality can be appropriate for this lesson and will change the nature of the inquiry and discussion.

CONCLUDING REMARKS

Active citizenship involves examining social issues by conducting historical inquiry and is the foundation of informed civic action. This lesson asks students and teachers to do this in a low-stakes way. Hopefully teachers and students will find the books *A Day in the Life of the Vice President* and *A Day in the Life of Marlon Bundo* accessible artifacts for discussing the current state, history, and ideology of marriage equality. The texts might stimulate intercultural conversations to personally analyze an important social issue. I suggest that the lesson may serve only as a beginning to this type of analysis.

Continual lessons and engagements of this type might lead to student development of increased critical literacy and discerning civic participation. Further, students will hopefully become better able to understand ways literature can be used as a mechanism for understanding and attending to civil rights.

Part of the process involves understanding literary concepts such as satire, hyperbole, caricature, and irony and how they can be part of our efforts to illuminate and challenge instances of social inequality.

Even if teachers decide not to consider this lesson as a whole, I recommend they (1) consider how they might use artifacts like *A Day in the Life of Marlon Bundo* to teach civic skills such as inquiry and historical thinking; (2) how the exchange of ideas might help stimulate dialogue for being a more active citizen; (3) and how a lesson like this can provide a shared experience for students to understand themselves as part of the enduring struggle for civil rights.

REFERENCES

Barton, K., & Levstik, L. (2004). *Teaching history for the common good*. Mahwah, NJ: Lawrence Erlbaum.

Blankenship, W. G., & Salinas, C. (2013). Shifting neo-narratives: Online participatory media & historical narrative. *Journal of the Research Center for Educational Technology, 9*(1), 74–93.

Freire, P. (2000). *Pedagogy of the oppressed* (30th aniv. ed.). New York: Bloomsbury Academic.

Kohl, H. (1994). Politics of children's literature: The Rosa Parks myth. *Rethinking Schools, 5*(2), 10–13.

Levstik, L. S., & Barton, K. C. (2011). *Doing history: Investigating with children in elementary and middle schools*. New York: Routledge.

Loewen, J. W. (2008). *Lies my teacher told me: Everything your American history textbook got wrong*. New York: New Press.

Magill, K. R. (2018). Critically civic teacher perception, posture, and pedagogy: Negating civic archetypes. *The Journal of Social Studies Research*. doi.org/10.1016/j.jssr.2018.09.005.

Naseem-Rodriguez, N. (2018). "Caught between two worlds": Asian American elementary teachers' enactment of Asian American history. *Educational Studies*, 1–26.

Roberts, P. (2000). *Education, literacy, and humanization: Exploring the work of Paulo Freire*. Santa Barbara, CA: Greenwood Publishing Group.

Rodriguez, A. (2008). Toward a transformative teaching practice: Criticity, pedagogy and praxis. *International Journal of Learning, 15*(3), 346–352.

Salinas, C., & Blevins, B. (2013). Enacting critical historical thinking: Decision making among preservice social studies teachers. *Teacher Education Quarterly, 40*(1), 7–24.

Salinas, C. S., Franquiz, M. E., & Naseem-Rodriguez, N. N. (2016). Writing Latina/o historical narratives: Narratives at the intersection of critical historical inquiry and LatCrit. *The Urban Review, 48*(2), 264–284.

Seixas, P., & Peck, C. (2004). Teaching historical thinking. In A. Sears & I. Wright (Eds.), *Challenges and prospects for Canadian social studies* (pp. 109–117). Vancouver: Pacific Educational Press.

Souto-Manning, M. (2010). *Freire, teaching, and learning: Culture circles across contexts*. New York: Peter Lang.

Stearns, P. N., Seixas, P. C., & Wineburg, S. (Eds.). (2000). *Knowing, teaching, and learning history: National and international perspectives*. New York: New York University Press.

VanSledright, B. (2002). *In search of America's past*. New York: Teachers College Press.

VanSledright, B. (2008). Narratives of nation-state, historical knowledge, and school history education. *Review of Research in Education, 32*(1), 109–146.

Vickery, A. E. (2017). "You excluded us for so long and now you want us to be patriotic?": African American women teachers navigating the quandary of citizenship. *Theory & Research in Social Education, 45*(3), 318–348.

Wineburg, S. (2001). *Historical thinking and other unnatural acts: Charting the future of teaching the past*. Philadelphia, PA: Temple University Press.

5

*Dreamers/*Soñadores

Exploring the Global Significance of Dreams and Activism through a Social Studies Lens

Sarah M. Straub

In this chapter, teachers will explore various ways to process Yuyi Morales's vivid personal story, *Dreamers/Soñadores*. The story shares Yuyi's trials and triumphs as she comes to the United States with her young son. It provides a humanizing way for students to process the political controversy revolving around immigration policy and allows students to deep dive into various NCSS themes relating to high-quality social studies instruction. Strong instruction allows students to develop meaningful connections with the content and to hone skills for democratic participation and activism. This chapter provides a structured way for students at various levels to engage in such practices.

BACKGROUND OF THE LITERATURE

Dreamers, winner of several awards including the *New York Times* Best Illustrated Book of 2018 and the 2019 Pura Belpré Illustrator Award, tells a story that is relevant and engaging for many students. It shares the story of making a home in a new place as a mother travels to the United States with her young child. And perhaps one of the most unique features of this particular book is that it is a true account from the author's own experiences! While creating a home is more of a universal theme, this story tackles the challenge of coming to the United States without English language proficiency. It shows how this family was able to push *adelante* (forward) by finding a connection with their public library.

In our social studies courses, we hope to learn about the push and pull factors that influence migration. Yet, in the United States, we have socially constructed both positive and negative definitions that have led to the development of a deficit mindset when applied to certain groups. Within the context of this story, the deficit mindset that is being challenged is that of the socially constructed idea of a Latin American immigrant having a negative impact on American society. The story moves beyond this deficit approach and shares what *migrantes* (migrants) bring with them when they enter the United States. They bring their dreams.

Included in the book are splendidly symbolic illustrations, a brief autobiographical essay from the author, and a list of supplemental resources for further learning. As this book will be connected to NCSS standards, each of these components will be useful as students explore current events and the volatile political climate for Dreamers to promote civic competence. An additional benefit of using this book is that even with the English version, *Dreamers*, various Spanish words are included. This provides the readers with an opportunity to develop an understanding of language differences/similarities and to grow their own language competency.

PEDAGOGICAL APPROACH

Teachers interested in engaging with this material must seek to adopt a culturally responsive pedagogical approach. Beyond "heroes and holidays," culturally *responsive* practices are actually *actions*. Teachers must actively get to know their students so they can include the students' stories in their classroom instruction. It focuses on both the successes and the failures of students through the lens of language interaction patterns between students and their teachers (Ladson-Billings, 1995).

To that effect, by focusing on students sharing personal connections and creating a space for collaboration and discussion over lecturing, the tasks described in this chapter align with culturally responsive practices. Other influential pedagogues support culturally responsive practices because these approaches honor students' experiences and introduce students to diverse authors and illustrators.

These practices only serve to build our students' capacity to learn (Hammond & Jackson, 2015). Additionally, one of the strongest methods to engage young students in culturally responsive ways is through the incorporation of stories. These stories require students to read, reflect, and build connections by incorporating their own cultural backgrounds and experiences (Irvine et al., 2000).

In addition to this pedagogical foundation, the teacher will need to have a working knowledge of project-based learning. More specifically, the teacher will need to know about the SAGE method of project-based learning. Students must "have opportunities to think deeply about issues of global significance" (Chowdhary, 2014).

The purpose of SAGE is to create projects/activities that address specific state standards but also increase a students' desire to act through the incorporation of four components: (1) Student Choice, (2) Authenticity, (3) Global Significance, and (4) Exhibition. "When it comes to student choice, the educator must give them an opportunity to opt-in or give them ownership of the project at least through some lens" (Straub, 2016).

In the case of *Dreamers*, students would connect based on family stories of immigration, although it is also critical to recognize our Native American students and their unique place in the "immigration story of America." At various points throughout these lessons, students are given opportunities to choose which books inspire them and why.

Projects that lend themselves to authenticity are ones that prepare students to have an increased role in our democratic society. To this effect, students would need to engage in a critical examination of the communities in which they live and identify opportunities for growth or examples to celebrate. This pairs nicely with the global significance portion of SAGE. Students will be asked to create something that is globally significant—their plans to address fairness or proposals for updated immigration policies fit in nicely here.

Lastly, exhibition allows students to present their learning to external audiences (Straub, 2016). This shows students that there is a greater purpose to their work. Each of these assignments can be extended to move beyond their own classrooms. While each level of students begins with a reading of *Dreamers/Soñadores* and various activities guide the students forward, each level culminates with an opportunity to "exhibit" their learning.

Lesson Objectives

When developing these series of lessons, it is first important for the reader to understand the perspective from which I develop curriculum. The National Council for Social Studies (NCSS) provides both curriculum and content standards. Content standards are the ones most of us are more familiar with (e.g., standards for civics, history, economics, geography, etc.). However, NCSS curriculum standards instead look at the pedagogical framework from which teachers implement these content standards.

As the NCSS states, "The civic mission of social studies require more than the acquisition of content. Since social studies has as its primary goal the development of a democratic citizenry, the experiences students have in their social studies classrooms should enable learners to engage in civic discourse and problem-solving, and to take informed civic action" (NCSS, 1994).

Table 5.1. Lesson Objectives

	NCSS Standard (Curriculum)[1]	Objectives
Elementary	Theme 1. Culture: Interact with class members and discover culturally based likenesses and differences. Theme 5. Individuals, Groups, and Institutions: Examine institutions that affect their lives and their thinking. Theme 6. Power, Authority, and Governance: Explore concepts of fairness, rights and responsibilities. Theme 10. Civic Ideals and Practices: Set classroom expectations, participate in mock elections, and determine how to balance the needs of the individual and the group.	SWBAT **define** culture. SBWAT **list** ways they are culturally similar to and different from their classmates. SWBAT **describe** individuals and groups that affect their lives. SWBAT **examine** fairness and unfairness. SWBAT **formulate** a plan that promotes fairness for all students in their classroom. **Deliverable(s):** Unfair to Fair Plan and Voting Scenario (described below)
Middle	Theme 1. Culture: Explore and ask questions about various cultures; analyze the influence of culture on human behavior. Theme 5. Individuals, Groups, and Institutions: Examine how institutions change over time and influence culture. Suggest ways to work through institutional change for the common good. Theme 6. Power, Authority, and Governance: Evaluate rights and responsibilities through a power lens. Theme 10. Civic Ideals and Practices: Apply concepts of civic involvement through participation in their communities.	SWBAT **define** culture. SWBAT **analyze** the influence of culture on human behavior. SBWAT **compare** institutional policies throughout American history that are directed at immigrant populations. SWBAT **examine** current policies for Dreamers. SWBAT **generate** a plan to participate in their community. **Deliverable(s):** Cultural Iceberg Activity, History of Immigration Gallery Walk, Fair/Unfair Immigration Law Scenario

| **Secondary** | Theme 1. Culture: Use cultural concepts like adaptation, assimilation, acculturation, diffusion, and dissonance. Theme 5. Individuals, Groups, and Institutions: Analyze the traditions that undergird social and political institutions. Examine social theory in relation to ways people and groups organize themselves around common needs, beliefs, and interests. Theme 6. Power, Authority, and Governance: Apply their knowledge and skills to participate in the workings of the various levels of power, authority, and governance. Theme 10. Civic Ideals and Practices: Become familiar with methods of analyzing important public issues and evaluating different recommendations for dealing with these issues. | SWBAT **analyze** Dreamers for examples of adaptation, assimilation, acculturation, diffusion, and dissonance. SWBAT **investigate** rationales behind government legislation specifically dealing with immigrants throughout American history. SWBAT **evaluate** different recommendations for Dreamers and **formulate** their own plan for action. **Deliverable(s):** Text Analysis Handout, History of Immigration Gallery Walk, Drafting a Bill, Voting Scenario |

1 Language taken directly from NCSS website: www.socialstudies.org/standards/strands

Content Overview

The foundational text *Dreamers/Soñadores* will serve as an introduction for the students to a specific immigration story from the perspective of a mother with her child who comes to the United States without a functional knowledge of English. Dependent on the group of learners the teacher has, this story will resonate on different levels. At the most basic, it is the story of family, and it is the story of creating a home. It is also a story of resiliency and problem solving. However, if the students come from immigrant backgrounds (and are potentially *undocumented* immigrants), this story can be profoundly triggering. The teacher should *know* the class before beginning this exploration.

There are three fundamental themes that this story allows students to explore at the elementary, middle, and secondary levels. These themes are culture (individuals, groups, and institutions); power, authority, and governance; and civic ideals and practices. Elementary students will explore their own cultural identity and then evaluate their classroom and community for examples of fairness and unfairness. Students will be expected to engage in conversations and develop a plan to address unfairness in their classroom spaces.

Middle school students will also explore cultural identity. They will examine pivotal examples of U.S. legislation geared toward immigrants and explore the current political situation for Dreamers in greater detail. They will then create a plan to engage with their community about this topic.

Secondary students will also explore the historical patterns of immigration policy in the United States before critically examining multiple perspectives on legislation geared toward Dreamers. They will formulate their own plan for action based on needs, beliefs, and common interests.

Materials/Supplies

- Morales, Yuyi. (2018). *Dreamers*. New York: Neal Porter Books, Holiday House.
- Morales, Yuyi. (2018). *Soñadores*. New York: Neal Porter Books, Holiday House.
- Chart paper—for read-alouds
- Handout—Elementary Level (sample shown in Figure 5.1)
- Yay/Nay Cards (sample shown in Figure 5.2)
- Cultural Iceberg—Teacher Resource (Figure 5.3)
- Cultural Iceberg—Student Handout (sample shown in Figure 5.4)
- Markers
- Construction paper (middle school)

- Major U.S. Immigration Laws (1790–Present). Retrieved from https://www.migration policy.org/research/timeline-1790 (middle and secondary only)
- Agree/Disagree Handout (sample shown in Figure 5.5)
- Waters, Joanna. (2017, September 17). Newsela: What is DACA and who are the Dreamers? Newsela. Retrieved from newsela.com/read/lib-overview-daca-dreamers/id/35159/ (middle and secondary)
- Associated Press. (2017, April 25). Trump softens stand on "dreamers" but stays firm on building border wall. Newsela. Retrieved from newsela.com/read/trump-immigration-dreamers/id/29840/ (middle and secondary)
- Access to Internet
- Brainstorming to Write a Bill Handout (colganhs.pwcs.edu/UserFiles/Servers/Server_415472/File/Library/Brainstorming%20and%20Drafting%20a%20Bill.pdf)
- Textual Analysis Handout (sample shown in Figure 5.6)
- Writing a Bill Template (sample shown in Figure 5.7)

SEQUENCE OF ACTIVITIES

Elementary

Estimated time: three 35-minute class periods

Hook

The teacher will begin by asking the students if they remember having any dreams. Students share out loud and then the teacher will clarify that there are dreams you have when you are asleep and there are dreams you have when you are awake—things you wish and hope for. The teacher allows students to share out with a partner and then has a few students share with the whole group.

Activity No. 1: Read-Aloud

The teacher first leads students through an exploration of the cover—the characters, its nature. She asks the students how it makes them feel. Explain to students that when you dream, it gives you hope. Hope is what you need to make change in the world.

During the read-aloud, have students repeat the Spanish words. The teacher will guide students through difficult words like "resplendent," "bundled," "immigrants," "improbable," and "resilience." The teacher will ask who the author is, ask students how they feel at various points, ask how the mom might feel, ask where they think the characters are going. What might the bridge symbolize?

As the teacher reads, the teacher will have chart paper up that has descriptors of images from the story that share details about the first place (the mother and child's original home) and the second place (where the mother and child move). Afterward, the teacher will tell students that these are examples from our cultures.

The teacher will define culture as things that people from a certain group have in common (i.e., food, language, clothing, music, arts, customs, beliefs, etc.). Next, ask the students, "How are you similar to and different from the characters in the book? How are you similar to and different from your classmates?"

Activity No. 2: Fair vs. Unfair

Discuss with students:

- What does fair mean to you? What does unfair mean?
- What are examples in school of things that are fair/unfair?
- What are some other things that are fair/unfair?
- What do you do when things are unfair? What *can* you do?

Activity No. 3: Our Dreams

The teacher will model something that was fair/unfair from his/her experiences in elementary school (who got to eat outside, who got to play what games, etc.). Then the teacher will model what he or she could have done as a student. Students will work in small groups to determine something that is unfair in the classroom/school. Depending on the grade level, students may phonetically spell their writing. Students will also develop an image that describes the unfairness and their plan to change it. Students will participate in this activity using their Fair Handout (Figure 5.1).

Students will present their ideas to the class and then the class will vote on which one(s) they want to try in their own classrooms. Students will participate in this mock election using Yay/Nay cards (Figure 5.2). Students can do these in each of the elementary-grade-level classrooms and have a whole grade-level presentation on their suggestions.

One thing that is **NOT** fair is _____

_____

_____

We can help this by _____

_____

_____

Figure 5.1. "We Have the Power to Make Things Fair." Handout (Elementary Level)

Extension Activity: Reading and Writing Gives Us Power . . . Let's Go to the Library

The teacher says, "We are going to do what the mother and child did in the book. We will take a field trip to the school library [if you have one] or the public library [if you can coordinate a trip]." This is a great time to get kids and their parents to register for library cards (if they can).

Figure 5.2. "Yay or Nay!" Cards (Elementary and Secondary Levels)

The teacher will tell students that they are responsible for choosing three books each. One book will be based on an interest. Another book will be based on learning something completely new. The third book is one that a classmate recommends to them. Over the course of the next week (or another period of time based on the reading level of students), the students will record their takeaways and share what "power" they've gained with their classmates.

Middle

Estimated time: five to eight 35-minute class periods

Hook

The teacher will clarify that there are dreams people have when they are asleep and there are dreams people have when they are awake—things they wish and hope for. The teacher then allows students to share out loud with a partner and then has a few students share with the whole group.

Next, ask if students have examples of people throughout time (or current people) who have had a dream and worked to create change based on that dream. The easiest example is Martin Luther King Jr. Students may include examples like Congressional Representative Alexandria Ocasio-Cortez changing the minimum salary of all of the people who work for her to a living wage. (Note: This chapter was written in 2019.) The teacher then says, "When you dream, it gives you hope. Hope is what you need to make change in the world."

Activity No. 1: Read-Aloud

During the read-aloud, the teacher will have students repeat the Spanish words. The teacher will guide students through difficult words like "resplendent," "bundled," "immigrants," "improbable," and "resilience." The teacher will also ask who the author is, ask students how they feel at various points, ask how the mom might feel, and ask where they think the characters are going. What might the bridge symbolize?

As the teacher reads, he or she will have chart paper up that has descriptors of images from the story that share details about the first place (the mother and child's original home) and the second place (where the mother and child move). Afterward, the teacher will tell students that these are examples from our cultures. Define culture as things that people from a certain group have in common (i.e., food, language, clothing, music, arts, customs, beliefs, etc.). After the class has finished and generated the list, the teacher will ask students how these elements of the cultures influenced human behavior.

Activity No. 2: Cultural Iceberg

Students will be introduced to the idea of the cultural iceberg (Figure 5.3). They will be given a set period of time to complete their own (Figure 5.4). Students will be asked to list things that they are comfortable listing. Afterward, students will partner up at their tables to share how *one* of these items influences *how* they behave. A simple example would be a student identifying as Christian: "My Christian values mean that I try to be kind to everyone."

Activity No. 3: History of Immigration Policy

The teacher asks students about what they know about government. Various answers may include that it provides freedom, it provides security, and so on. The teacher connects to the story because of the power of dreams.

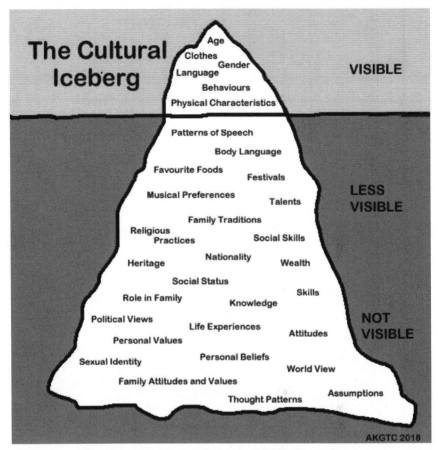

Figure 5.3. Cultural Iceberg Teacher Resource (Middle Level). *Image courtesy of A Kids' Guide to Canada. Text available under Public License: https://akgtcanada.com/ if-i-really-knew-you/.*

Throughout history, we've wanted to create an American Dream. What is that? What is "America"?

The teacher guides the conversation toward policy: "Our government passes laws to make our lives more secure. The ones we will focus on today are laws throughout history for immigration." The teacher will have accessed the document Major U.S. Immigration Laws (1790–Present) and cut each of the dates into strips. There are thirty-one different dates with the most recent one being 2006. The teacher may decide to select ten of the most pertinent ones (this may depend on school location and student demographics) or do all of them. The teacher will also tell students that they will be looking at more recent legislation in the next activity.

My Cultural Iceberg

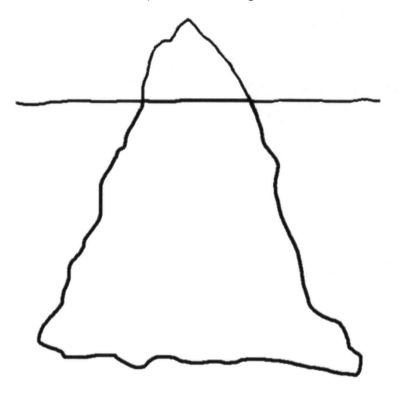

One element of my cultural iceberg is _____

_____

This influences HOW I behave because _____

_____

_____

_____

Figure 5.4.   Student's Cultural Iceberg Handout (Middle Level). *Author created.*

Students will then work in groups or independently to create a description and image of their event on construction paper. Students will then place their images in chronological order and then participate in a gallery walk. During this gallery walk, they are looking for examples of ideas they agree with and ideas that they don't agree with (Figure 5.5). Afterward, students will return

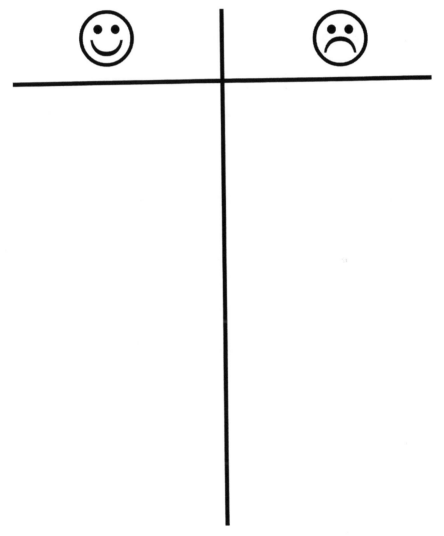

Figure 5.5. "Agree/Disagree" Student Handout (Middle and Secondary Level). *Author created.*

to small groups to share their ideas. Teacher may decide to have students engage in a whole group discussion as well.

Activity No. 4: Dreamers and DACA

Students will read through two Newsela sources. Newsela is a great resource for which teachers must register. A great part of this website is that the teacher can select various reading levels that have been adapted by Newsela staff so that all of the students in your classroom can read the same article at the appropriate reading level.

Students will divide into table groups. Half of the students will read the first Newsela article and the other half will read the other. Another way to modify it is to have the first reading be for homework and the second reading completed in class. Students will begin by journaling their main takeaways independently.

Afterward, students will need to access the Internet (BYOD, mobile labs, trip to the library, etc.). They will research organizations in their community that are focused on immigrant rights and look for events. If there are none, students will create a hypothetical plan for action, present it to the class, and then decide which plan should be sent to a local government official.

Extension Activity: Books That Inspired Me (and Still Do)

At the end of the book, Yuyi Morales includes a list of books that have inspired her. Have students look through this list. Based on titles, have them pull out one or two that they would be interested in reading and have them tell their tables (or the class) why.

Then, have students create their own list of five to ten books that have inspired them. They can create this on PowerPoint (or an equivalent platform). Students will have the title of the book, a one- or two-sentence summary, and then a longer reflection on *why/how* it inspired them. They will present their top book to the class, if time allows.

Secondary

Estimated time: five 35-minute class periods

Hook

The teacher will clarify that there are dreams you have when you are asleep and there are dreams you have when you are awake—things you wish and hope for. The teacher allows students to share out loud with a partner and then has a few students share with the whole group.

Next, ask students if they know examples of people throughout time (or current people) who have had a dream and worked to create change based on that dream. The easiest example is Martin Luther King Jr. Students may include examples like Congressional Representative Alexandria Ocasio-Cortez changing the minimum salary of all of the people who work for her to a living wage. (Note: This chapter was written in 2019). The teacher then says, "When you dream, it gives you hope. Hope is what you need to make change in the world."

Activity No. 1: Read-Aloud

During the read-aloud, the teacher will have students repeat the Spanish words. The teacher will guide students through difficult words like "resplendent", "bundled," "immigrants," "improbable," and "resilience." The teacher will ask who the author is, ask students how they feel at various points, ask how the mom might feel, and ask where they think the characters are going. What might the bridge symbolize?

Students will be reading this book independently or in groups. It can be accessed online for students who need to finish work at home. Over the course of the first class period, students will be analyzing the text for examples of adaption, assimilation, acculturation, and diffusion. Students may need a refresher on these definitions. Students will collect their responses on a Text Analysis Handout (Figure 5.6). Students may share out loud with partners, in groups, or as a whole class.

Activity No. 2: History of Immigration Policy

The teacher asks students about what they know about government. Various answers may include that it provides freedom, it provides security, and so on. The teacher connects to the story because of the power of dreams. Throughout history, we've wanted to create an American Dream. What is that? What is "America"?

The teacher then guides the conversation toward policy: "Our government passes laws to make our lives more secure. The ones we will focus on today are laws throughout history for immigration." The teacher will have accessed the document Major U.S. Immigration Laws (1790–Present) and cut each of the dates into strips. There are thirty-one different dates with the most recent one being 2006. The teacher may decide to select ten of the most pertinent ones (this may depend on school location and student demographics) or do all

Directions: As you read through the text, look for examples of adaptation, assimilation, and diffusion. Try to make a connection to current events.

Excerpt from Text	Analysis
Example: Thousands and thousands of steps we took around this land, until the day we found a place we had never seen before…	This is an example of adaptation because… they are in a library and they are spending time learning English. Adapting means that you adjust to new conditions.
	This is an example of assimilation because…
	This is an example of diffusion because…
	This connects to current events because…

Figure 5.6.   Sample Textual Analysis Handout (Secondary Level). *Author created.*

of them. The teacher will also tell students that they will be looking at more recent legislation in the next activity.

Students will work in groups or independently to create a description and image of their event on construction paper. Students will then place their images in chronological order and then participate in a gallery walk. During this gallery walk, they are looking for examples of ideas they agree with and ideas that they don't agree with (Figure 5.5).

Afterward, students will return to small groups to share their ideas. The teacher may decide to have students engage in a whole group discussion as well. Focus the conversation on *why* these policies may have passed. Have students note *one* policy that they were confused about. That is a policy they will research for homework that evening (or in class, if time allows).

Activity No. 3: Dreamers and DACA

Students will read through two Newsela sources. Newsela is a great resource for which teachers must register. A great part of this website is that the teacher can select various reading levels that have been adapted by Newsela staff so that all of the students in your classroom can read the same article at the appropriate reading level. Students will divide into table groups.

Half of the students will read the first Newsela article, and the other half will read the other. Another way to modify it is to have the first reading be for homework and the second reading completed in class. Students will begin by journaling their main takeaways independently.

Afterward, students will need to access the Internet (BYOD, mobile labs, trip to the library, etc.). They will research various perspectives on recommended legislation as it relates to Dreamers. In addition to the two sources they've already read, the group must have the following sources in their research collection:

- Personal account from a Dreamer
- Article from Obama administration on Dreamers and Dream Act
- Article from Trump administration on Dreamers and Dream Act

Next, students will work in groups to formulate their own proposed plan of action. (Use the Brainstorming to Write a Bill Handout to guide their discussions [Figure 5.7].) Students will present their bills to the class. The class will participate in a mock voting session using Yay/Nay cards (Figure 5.2). These suggestions may be community specific, and the top suggestions can be sent to local government officials.

Extension Activity: Books That Inspired Me (and Still Do)

At the end of the book, Yuyi Morales includes a list of books that have inspired her. Have students look through this list. Based on titles, have them

A Bill to _____

The Enactment Clause

Be it enacted by the Senate and House of Representatives of the United States of America in Congress assembled, that ...

_____

_____

The Body of Your Legislation

Section 1: Main effect of the legislation

1. _____

_____

2. _____

_____

3. _____

_____

Section 2: Limitations and restrictions

1. _____

_____

2. _____

_____

Section 3: Cost/Penalties or fines

1. _____

_____

2. _____

_____

3. _____

_____

Section 4: Date of Effect

This bill will be enacted on _____

---

[1] Adapted from: http://www.congresslink.org/print_lp_mocksenatesimulation_wtb.htm#sthash.kk1bJZFj.dpuf and http://www.ehow.com/how_7554583_write-billstudent-congress-competition.html

Figure 5.7. Brainstorming to Write a Bill Handout (Secondary Level). Adapted from http://www.congresslink.org/print_lp_mocksenatesimulation_wtb/htm#sthash. kk1bJZFj.dpuf and http://www.ehow.com/how_7554583_write-billstudent-congress-competition.html.

pull out one or two that they would be interested in reading and have them tell their tables (or the class) why.

Next, have students create their own list of five to ten books that have inspired them. They can create this on PowerPoint (or an equivalent platform). Students will have the title of the book, a one- or two-sentence summary, and then a longer reflection on *why/how* it inspired them. They will present their top book to the class, if time allows.

Tips for Struggling/Reluctant Readers

One option for struggling and reluctant readers is to provide them the option of accessing the story by having it read to them in a video. One example of this is found in a YouTube video that you can access here: www.youtube. com/watch?v=jPuI4LEQf3M. Additionally, to make this text more accessible to readers, the teacher must explicitly model skills of proficient readers including reading with fluency and expression.

Tips for English Language Learners/Emergent Bilinguals

A useful tip for engaging with emergent bilingual populations is to build bridges with students' home language(s) (Cain, 2018). The majority "second language" in the United States is Spanish, so the book *Dreamers* being available in Spanish presents an opportunity for newly emergent bilingual students to engage with the text in Spanish. The *Dreamers* text in its original form includes various Spanish words that may make the text more accessible as well.

Another tip for engaging with emergent bilingual students is to understand language development. For the most part, when learning a second language, the learner is comfortable reading and/or writing before they are comfortable engaging in an academic conversation out loud. A way to minimize the stress of oral communication is to allow students to speak with a partner rather than the whole group and to allow communication in both languages.

Evaluation of Skills

Each figure includes a student handout or teacher resource. While these are left blank, the teachers can see a clear progression of learning for each of the objectives noted in the earlier sections of this chapter. The teachers have the flexibility to modify texts to more directly reflect issues in their own communities.

Additional Online Resources

- Kleinrock, Liz. *How to teach kids to talk about taboo topics.* www.you tube.com/watch?v=G9-urSR19SI
  Teachers can use this resource to learn specific ways to discuss taboo topics with elementary school students without fear. She focuses on racism while these lessons focus on immigration, but the pedagogical takeaways are similar.
- *Dreamers by Yuyi Morales: An interactive read aloud book for kids.* www.youtube.com/watch?v=jPuI4LEQf3M
  This resource can be shared with parents if they want to see what their students are reading. It can also be used to help students who may need to revisit the text at a later date or students who were absent from the first day of instruction for this unit.
- www.newsela.com
  Newsela is a resource that can only be accessed once a teacher has created a free profile. The benefit of this resource is that it provides leveled texts that have been adapted from news sources like the Associated Press and the *New York Times* for various reading levels. It also provides some options for reading comprehension support.

CONCLUDING REMARKS

Education is meant to provide students with the skills they need to critically examine their lives and the world around them. This chapter provided a structure that teachers can implement in which students are provided with structures to have a voice. Students learn the required academic vocabulary, apply it within the context of the story, and then extend the themes addressed in the story to their own communities in an active way.

The lessons in this chapter directly relate to the following NCSS themes:

1. Culture;
5. Individuals, Groups, and Institutions;
6. Power, Authority, and Governance; and
10. Civic Ideals and Practices.

Students are analyzing their culturally based likenesses and differences with the Cultural Iceberg Activity and with text analysis. Students are examining the institutions that have profound impacts on their thinking when they learn about the history of immigration law in the United States. Students explore concepts of fairness, rights, and responsibilities as they analyze the story and analyze the laws they've explored. Lastly, students practice their civic ideals in mock classroom proceedings and with exhibitions to grade levels, community members, and politicians.

The use of a multicultural text like *Dreamers* allows students to explore an issue from the perspective of the immigrant experience. It humanizes this topic in a way that just looking at legislation does not. When students humanize, when *we* humanize, we begin to practice the skills that allow us to empathize and to critically think about the implication of our choices for various groups—not just for the groups with whom we identify.

REFERENCES

Cain, A. A. (2018). Seven tips for teachers of newcomer emergent bilingual students. *The Reading Teacher, 71*(4), 485–490. Retrieved from ila.onlinelibrary.wiley.com/doi/pdf/10.1002/trtr.1648

Chowdhary, N. (2014). Global competence: A "SAGE" approach to project-based learning (deeper learning). *Teaching Channel.* Retrieved from www.teachingchannel.org/blog/2014/06/04/sage-approach-to-project-based-learning

Hammond, Z., & Jackson, Y. (2015). *Culturally responsive teaching and the brain: Promoting authentic engagement and rigor among culturally and linguistically diverse students.* Thousand Oaks, CA: Corwin.

Irvine, J., Armento, B., Causey, C., Jones, J., Frasher, R., & Weinburgh, M. (2000). *Culturally responsive teaching: Lesson planning for elementary and middle grades.* Thousand Oaks, CA: Corwin.

Ladson-Billings, G. (1995). Toward a theory of culturally relevant pedagogy. *American Educational Research Journal, 32*(3), 466–491. Retrieved from lmcreadinglist.pbworks.com/f/Ladson-Billings%20%281995%29.pdf

Morales, Y. (2018). *Dreamers.* New York: Neal Porter Books, Holiday House.

Morales, Y. (2018). *Soñadores.* New York: Neal Porter Books, Holiday House.

National Council for the Social Studies (1994). *Expectations of excellence: Curriculum standards for social studies.* Washington, DC: National Council for the Social Studies.

Straub, S. M. (2016). The mothers of exiles: Authentic project-based learning in a social studies classroom. *MLET: The Journal of Middle Level Education, 3*(1). Retrieved from scholarworks.sfasu.edu/cgi/viewcontent.cgi?article=1008&context=mlet

Section Two

USING MULTICULTURAL LITERATURE
FOR SCIENCE AND MATHEMATICS

6

Black Pioneers of Science and Invention

Exploring the Impact of Black Scientists on the Field Today

Yasmin C. Laird

In the text *Black Pioneers of Science and Invention*, authored by Louis Haber, the influence of black American scientists is examined, illuminating the impact of their crucial contributions to scientific progress today. The text not only communicates the interest of each scientist but also their fields of study and how each scientist and inventor was able to save lives, improve jobs, and change the course of history. Furthermore, Haber celebrates the work and inventions of black Americans, thus inspiring young people of all ethnicities and cultures of their potential and possibilities to make a difference in their lives and the lives of others, regardless of their social, cultural, linguistic, or economic backgrounds.

Organized in a chapter-book style, *Black Pioneers of Science and Invention* uses outstanding research conducted by the author to examine each scientist and inventor in depth. This analysis engages students with each individual from the text—beginning with the background information on each scientist, and moving on to their inventions and the impact of their developments. Though their contributions may not have received much recognition in their lifetimes, *Black Pioneers* precisely demonstrates the works of individuals from different backgrounds, cultures, and races and how they are often undervalued, discounted, or overlooked, though their contributions have shaped the world we know today.

In this lesson, students will examine various black scientists and their lives, contributions, and impacts through a series of activities and experiments. Beginning with a read-aloud, the teacher and students will engage in thoughtful discussion and inquiry, leading to researching, investigating, presenting, and experimenting.

BACKGROUND OF THE LITERATURE

Black Pioneers of Science and Invention by Louis Haber is a work of nonfiction aimed at illuminating the inventions and contributions of African Americans, ranging from the eighteenth to twentieth centuries. Reprinted in 1992, this timeless and informative text offers a perceptive account on the history and the lives of fourteen gifted black innovators, complete with their additions to scientific and industrial progress. Throughout the text, Haber calls attention to the notion that even though the achievements of these pioneers are known worldwide, the scientists themselves are seldom recognized.

A great deal of the text is designed to capture the interest and attention of readers of all ages. Through thought-provoking examples of milestones in science, such as the very first open-heart surgery and the invention of the gas mask, the book focuses on a variety of notable pioneers. These scientists include, but are not limited to, Benjamin Banneker, Granville T. Woods, George Washington Carver, and others who have all made jobs easier, saved lives, and altered the course of history as a whole.

Haber does a satisfactory job in making each of the pioneers feel like tangible characters through the great deal of interesting background information presented in the book. With the author's background in education and science, Haber saw a clear deficit in information on the impact that African American inventors and scientists have had on the world today.

Haber's book not only engages readers of all ages but informs all on these remarkable contributors to science. Chapters in this text could be conducive and advantageous in a multicultural science curriculum across all grade levels.

PEDAGOGICAL APPROACH

This chapter proposes an inquiry circle model and project-based learning approach to a variety of science lessons and activities. Through inquiry circles, students are able to have a vessel for fostering authentic conversations about a text. These discussions allow for discovery in the sciences, as well as time for teachers to get to know their students and their personal connections to the content.

Over the years, many studies have been conducted across all grade levels on how using inquiry circles can help students determine main ideas, make comparisons and connections, discover cause-and-effect relationships, summarize, make predictions, draw conclusions, make generalizations, pose questions, visualize the text through mental imagery, determine importance, and synthesize the text (Harvey & Daniels, 2009; TEA, 2016; Tompkins, 2014).

Furthermore, by focusing on students sharing personal connections through inquiry circles and creating a space for collaboration and discussion, the tasks described in this chapter align with culturally responsive practices.

Additionally, by integrating project-based learning into the lesson, students are sustained in motivation and thought. Through project-based learning, students are not only engaged but also are given the potential for investigation of authentic problems and concepts (Blumenfeld et al., 1991). Project-based activities, such as those outlined in the SAGE method, should allow for (1) Student Choice, (2) Authenticity, (3) Global Significance, and (4) Exhibition, which in turn grant a classroom "opportunities to think deeply about issues of global significance" (Chowdhary, 2014). Finally, through culturally responsive pedagogy implemented through the use of this book, the text and corresponding activities create relevance to many of the students' lives and experiences (Howard, 2012).

By creating a learning environment that allows students to utilize cultural, linguistic, and identity-defining elements, as well as other recognizable knowledge that the students are familiar with, the vast door of opportunity to learn new content and information is opened in order to enhance students' schooling experience and academic success.

Lesson Objectives

Before implementing these lessons in a classroom, one must understand the foundation from which the activities are developed. The National Science Education Standards provide a comprehensive guide for not only standards on science curriculum, but also standards for science content and assessment. These standards include a range of specific branches of science, from physical, earth, space, and life science, to science in technology, inquiry, history, social, and personal perspectives (see Table 6.1).

Content Overview

In these lessons, inspired by the information in *Black Pioneers of Science and Invention* by Louis Haber, students will be introduced to specific examples of black scientists and their contributions to the field today. Dependent on the group of learners you have, the stories from the scientists will resonate on different levels (based on student backgrounds, experiences, and interests).

Table 6.1. Lesson Objectives

	National Science Education Standards	Objectives
Elementary	**1. Inquiry:** Combine scientific reasoning and critical thinking to develop student understanding of science. **5. Science & Technology:** Establish connections between the natural and designed worlds. **6. Personal & Social Perspectives:** Give students a means to understand and act on personal and social issues. **7. History:** Understand how science reflects its history and is an ongoing, changing enterprise.	SWBAT **identify** fourteen African American inventors and scientists through reading and conducting research on each figure. SWBAT **distinguish** between natural objects and objects made by humans (black scientists). SBWAT **describe** ways they are culturally similar to and different from the scientists, as well as the challenges the scientists have faced. SWBAT **examine** the inventor/scientist's contribution to society and provide a brief biography on their life.
Middle	**1. Inquiry:** Combine scientific reasoning and critical thinking to develop student understanding of science. **5. Science & Technology:** Establish connections between the natural and designed worlds. **6. Personal & Social Perspectives:** Give students a means to understand and act on personal and social issues. **7. History:** Understand how science reflects its history and is an ongoing, changing enterprise.	SWBAT **identify** fourteen African American inventors and scientists through reading and researching each figure, as well as conducting experiments relevant to the scientists. SWBAT **distinguish** between natural objects and objects made by humans (black scientists). SBWAT **describe** ways they are culturally similar to and different from the scientists, as well as the challenges the scientists have faced. SWBAT **examine** the inventor/scientist's contribution to society and provide a brief biography on their life.

Secondary

1. Inquiry:
Combine scientific reasoning and critical thinking to develop student understanding of science.

5. Science & Technology:
Establish connections between the natural and designed worlds.

6. Personal & Social Perspectives:
Give students a means to understand and act on personal and social issues.

7. History:
Understand how science reflects its history and is an ongoing, changing enterprise.

SWBAT **identify** fourteen African American inventors and scientists through reading and researching each figure, as well as conducting experiments relevant to the scientists.

SWBAT **distinguish** between natural objects and objects made by humans (black scientists).

SBWAT **describe** ways they are culturally similar to and different from the scientists, as well as the challenges the scientists have faced.

SWBAT **examine** the inventor/scientist's contribution to society and provide a brief biography on their life.

Across the elementary, middle, and secondary levels, students will focus on the themes of inquiry, science and technology, history, and personal and social perspectives. These themes are culture; individuals, groups, and institutions; power, authority and governance; and civic ideals and practices.

Elementary students will explore the role of humans in the development of science with an emphasis on the importance of African American scientists in the progression of scientific and industrial advances. Students will be expected to engage in research, conversations, and experiments pertinent to their black scientists.

Middle school students will also explore these facets of black scientists, as well as conduct deeper, more detailed experiments. Secondary students will also explore the aforementioned details, as well as partake in higher-level experiments featuring electrical circuits.

Materials/Supplies

- Haber, Louis. (1992). *Black pioneers of science and invention*. Orlando, FL: Odyssey Classic/Harcourt.
- Computers or devices with Internet access
- Library books and encyclopedias
- Graphic organizers
- Notebooks and paper
- Writing utensils
- Poster board, scissors, glue
- Markers
- Milk jugs
- Red, green, and yellow cellophane
- Christmas lights—white, red, green, and yellow
- Aluminum foil cut into strips
- Brass brads
- Tape
- 9-volt batteries
- Chart paper—for read-alouds
- Scientist "Who am I" student copy—elementary and middle school level (Table 6.3)
- Scientist "Who am I" teacher copy—elementary and middle school level (Table 6.4)
- Circuit Experiment Student Handout (Figure 6.1)
- List of scientists, including women not mentioned in the book (Table 6.2)

SEQUENCE OF ACTIVITIES

Elementary

Estimated time: three 35-minute class periods

Hook

The teacher will begin by asking the students for examples of science and inventions. Students will share with a partner, and then a few students will share with the whole group. The teacher will then transition the conversation to ask the students about the differences between science created by nature and science created by scientists.

Discuss as a class how science has changed our world, how scientists have made contributions, and how African American scientists may have had to face different obstacles to make their contributions to science.

Activity No. 1: Read-Aloud

The teacher will ask students who the author is. While reading, ask students how they feel about the scientists at various points. If they were a scientist, what would they invent? What and who would this invention benefit? If they invented something, what obstacles would they potentially face? How would they feel if they went through the same struggles as these scientists?

After reading the text, the students will break into inquiry circles, choosing one or more scientists to focus on (this can be done over one or multiple class days/lessons). As the book is read, students will keep a log of special information pertaining to each scientist. The students will work together toward determining the text's main ideas, discovering cause-and-effect relationships, and making predictions and conclusions.

Activity No. 2: African American Scientists, Innovators, and Engineers "Who Am I?"

On a sheet of paper, list the names of the African American scientists that the students have studied, as well as one sentence per scientist describing the contribution, invention, or accomplishment that he/she made. The students will match the scientist to the statement, filling in the blank. This activity can also be done in group inquiry circles.

Based on the information from the text, students can work together toward determining the text's main ideas, discovering cause-and-effect relationships, and making predictions and conclusions in order to gain understanding on the

Table 6.2. Suggested List of Black Scientists

Benjamin Banneker
Norbert Rillieux
Jan Earnst Matzeliger
Elijah McCoy
Granville T. Woods
Lewis Howard Latimer
Garrett A. Morgan
George Washington Carver
Percy Lavon Julian
Lloyd A. Hall
Ernest Everett Just
Daniel Hale Williams
Louis Tompkins Wright
Charles Richard Drew
Alice Ball
Katherine Johnson
Claudia Alexander
Lilia Ann Abron

scientists from the book. *Note:* The handout from Table 6.3 includes black female scientists that were not mentioned in the book. In order to avoid gender bias, take some time to brief the students on these scientists.

Activity No. 3: Presentation

Students, working either individually, in pairs, or in groups, will select a scientist, engineer, or inventor of color to study. Students should be encouraged to research information on their individual via websites, library books, and other resources. The students will then transfer the information to a drawing, story, graphic organizer, or other format depending on grade level. The students will present the information to the class and teacher, and the teacher may or may not create a rubric for grading. Students can do these in each of the elementary-grade-level classrooms and have a whole-grade-level presentation on their scientists.

Activity No. 4: Experiment—Chemical Stoplight

As a class, discuss Garrett A. Morgan, the inventor of the traffic light. Discuss the importance of stoplights in our world today. Ask students for predictions on how a traffic light could be made.

Prepare materials, divide students into groups, and walk students through the following steps:

Table 6.3. Who am I? (Elementary and Middle School Level) STUDENT COPY. Match the Scientist to Their Description!

Benjamin Banneker	He researched in the field of blood transfusions, developed improved techniques for blood storage, and applied his expert knowledge to developing large-scale blood banks early in World War II.
Norbert Rillieux	First African American woman to earn a PhD in chemical engineering.
Jan Earnst Matzeliger	An engineer who was notable for his fifty-seven U.S. patents, most having to do with the lubrication of steam engines.
Elijah McCoy	The inventor of the stoplight, the smoke hood, and chemical hair-straightening solutions.
Granville T. Woods	A research chemist and a pioneer in the chemical synthesis of medicinal drugs from plants.
Lewis Howard Latimer	Mathematician whose calculations of orbital mechanics as a NASA employee were critical to the success of the first and subsequent U.S. manned spaceflights.
Garrett A. Morgan	The first American of African ancestry to be a mechanical and electrical engineer after the Civil War. Self-taught, he concentrated most of his work on trains and streetcars.
George Washington Carver	The first African American on the surgical staff of a nonsegregated hospital in New York City.
Percy Lavon Julian	First woman and African American to receive a master's degree from the University of Hawaii.
Lloyd A. Hall	An inventor whose lasting machine brought significant change to the manufacturing of shoes.
Ernest Everett Just	He is one of the earliest chemical engineers and noted for his pioneering invention of the multiple-effect evaporator.
Daniel Hale Williams	An African American engineer and inventor who was a member of Thomas Edison's research team, which was called "Edison's Pioneers."
Louis Tompkins Wright	Project manager for NASA's Galileo mission and Rosetta mission.
Charles Richard Drew	The inventor of alternative crops to cotton and methods to prevent soil depletion.
Alice Ball	American general surgeon, who in 1893 performed the first documented successful pericardium surgery in the United States to repair a wound.
Katherine Johnson	The inventor of America's first clock.
Claudia Alexander	His primary legacy is his recognition of the fundamental role of the cell surface in the development of organisms.
Lilia Ann Abron	A chemist who contributed to the science of food preservation.

Table 6.4.   Who am I? (Elementary and Middle School Level) TEACHER COPY. Match the Scientist to Their Description!

Benjamin Banneker	He researched in the field of blood transfusions, developed improved techniques for blood storage, and applied his expert knowledge to developing large-scale blood banks early in World War II. (Charles R. Drew)
Norbert Rillieux	First African American woman to earn a PhD in chemical engineering. (Lilia Ann Abron)
Jan Earnst Matzeliger	An engineer who was notable for his fifty-seven U.S. patents, most having to do with the lubrication of steam engines. (Elijah McCoy)
Elijah McCoy	The inventor of the stoplight, the smoke hood, and chemical hair-straightening solutions. (Garrett A. Morgan)
Granville T. Woods	A research chemist and a pioneer in the chemical synthesis of medicinal drugs from plants. (Percy Lavon Julian)
Lewis Howard Latimer	Mathematician whose calculations of orbital mechanics as a NASA employee were critical to the success of the first and subsequent U.S. manned spaceflights. (Katherine Johnson)
Garrett A. Morgan	The first American of African ancestry to be a mechanical and electrical engineer after the Civil War. Self-taught, he concentrated most of his work on trains and streetcars. (Granville T. Woods)
George Washington Carver	The first African American on the surgical staff of a nonsegregated hospital in New York City. (Louis T. Wright)
Percy Lavon Julian	First woman and African American to receive a master's degree from the University of Hawaii. (Alice Ball)
Lloyd A. Hall	An inventor whose lasting machine brought significant change to the manufacturing of shoes. (Jan Earnst Matzeliger)
Ernest Everett Just	He is one of the earliest chemical engineers and noted for his pioneering invention of the multiple-effect evaporator. (Norbert Rillieux)
Daniel Hale Williams	An African American engineer and inventor who was a member of Thomas Edison's research team, which was called "Edison's Pioneers." (Lewis Howard Latimer)
Louis Tompkins Wright	Project manager for NASA's Galileo mission and Rosetta mission. (Claudia Alexander)
Charles Richard Drew	The inventor of alternative crops to cotton and methods to prevent soil depletion. (George Washington Carver)
Alice Ball	American general surgeon, who in 1893 performed the first documented successful pericardium surgery in the United States to repair a wound. (Daniel Hale Williams)
Katherine Johnson	The inventor of America's first clock. (Benjamin Banneker)
Claudia Alexander	His primary legacy is his recognition of the fundamental role of the cell surface in the development of organisms. (Ernest Everett Just)
Lilia Ann Abron	A chemist who contributed to the science of food preservation. (Lloyd Hall)

1. Pour 125ml of water into a bottle.
2. Pour 5 drops of blue food coloring into the bottle.
3. The teacher will walk around the classroom giving each bottle 2.5g of sodium hydroxide and 1.5g glucose.
4. Watch the "stoplight" turn from red, to yellow, to green!

Extension Activity: Library and Inventions

The students will take a field trip to the school library (if you have one) or the public library (if you can coordinate a trip). This is a great time to get kids and their parents to register for library cards (if they can). The teacher will tell students that they are responsible for choosing a book about a scientist or an invention they find interesting. They will read the book, either alone or in pairs, noting important information about the scientist, their background, their inventions, and their impact on science as a whole. After reading the book, the students will pair up to share what they learned. Students can also brainstorm an invention they would like to create someday.

Middle

Estimated time: five to eight 35-minute class periods

Hook

The teacher will begin by asking the students for examples of science and inventions. The teacher allows students to share with a partner and then has a few students share with the whole group, then transitions the conversation to ask the students about the differences between science created by nature and science created by scientists.

Discuss as a class how science has changed our world, how scientists have made contributions, and how African American scientists may have had to face different obstacles than white scientists in order to make their contributions to science.

Activity No. 1: Read-Aloud

Ask students who the author is. While reading, ask students how they feel about the scientists at various points. If they were a scientist, what would they invent? How would the world be better with this invention? What would it take to create and implement this invention? What obstacles could they face with this invention? Would this invention receive any backlash from anyone? How would they feel if they went through the same struggles as these scientists?

After reading the text, the students will break into inquiry circles, choosing one or more scientists to focus on (this can be done over one or multiple class days/lessons). As the book is read, students will keep a log of special information pertaining to each scientist. The students will work together toward determining the text's main ideas, discovering cause-and-effect relationships, and making predictions and conclusions.

After you've finished and generated the list, ask students how these black scientists influenced scientists who came after them.

Activity No. 2: African American Scientists, Innovators, and Engineers "Who Am I?"

On a sheet of paper, list the names of the African American scientists that the students have studied, as well as one sentence per scientist describing the contribution, invention, or accomplishment that he/she made. The students will match the scientist to the statement, filling in the blank. This activity can also be done in group inquiry circles.

Based on the information from the text, students can work together toward determining the text's main ideas, discovering cause-and-effect relationships, and making predictions and conclusions in order to gain understanding on the scientists from the book.

Note: The handout from Table 6.3 includes black female scientists that were not mentioned in the book. In order to avoid gender bias, take some time to brief the students on these scientists.

Activity No. 3: Presentation

Students, working either individually, in pairs, or in groups, will select a scientist, engineer, or inventor of color to study. Students should be encouraged to research information on their individual via websites, library books, and other resources.

The students will then transfer the information to a PowerPoint presentation. On the presentation, the students should include information on who the scientist is, why they were selected, their contributions to science, the time period in which they lived and how this time period played a role in the scientist's achievements, any obstacles the scientist faced, and so on (including references).

The students will present the information to the class and teacher, and the teacher may or may not create a rubric for grading. Students can do these in each of their grade level's science classrooms/periods and have a whole grade-level presentation on their scientists *or* they can display their scientist's information around the classroom or hallway for other class periods to see.

Activity No. 4: Electrical Stoplight

As a class, discuss Garrett A. Morgan, the inventor of the traffic light. Discuss the importance of stoplights in our world today. Ask students for predictions on how a traffic light could be made.

Prepare materials, divide students into groups, and walk students through the following steps:

1. Cut three holes into a half-gallon milk carton. The holes should be 3 inches wide and at least 1 inch apart. Center the circles from left to right and top to bottom on the carton. Line the inside of the carton with black paper or (optional) paint the milk jug with black paint.
2. Cut a circle from each color of cellophane that is slightly larger than the holes in the milk carton. A standard stoplight needs one red, one amber (orange), and one green circle.
3. Glue the cellophane to the inside of the carton. Glue the red circle inside the top circle, the yellow in the middle, and the green in the bottom circle. Set aside to dry.
4. Lay the milk carton down on the work surface with the "lights" up. Place the holiday light string inside so that one light is behind each circle. Test the lights to ensure they light in sequence to mimic a real traffic light. Allow the rest of the string to dangle down out of the milk carton. Use masking tape to secure the string of lights in place.
5. Enjoy watching the stoplight come to life!

Secondary

Estimated time: five 35-minute class periods

Hook

The teacher will begin by asking the students for examples of science and inventions. The teacher allows students to share with a partner and then has a few students share with the whole group, The teacher then transitions the conversation to ask the students about the differences between science created by nature and science created by scientists.

What is a Simple Circuit?

❖ Simple Circuit

A simple circuit consists of three elements: a source of electricity (battery), a path or conductor on which electricity flows (wire), and a electrical resistor (lamp) which is any device that requires electricity to operate. The illustration below shows a simple circuit containing a battery, two wires, and a low voltage light bulb. The flow of electricity is caused by excess electrons on the negative end of the battery flowing toward the positive end, or terminal, of the battery. When the circuit is complete, electrons flow from the negative terminal through the wire conductor, then through the bulb (lighting it up), and finally back to the positive terminal – in a continual flow.

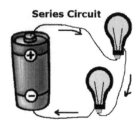

❖ Schematic Diagram of a Simple Circuit

The following is a schematic diagram of the simple circuit showing the electronic symbols for the battery, switch, and bulb.

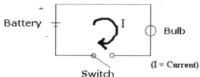

Figure 6.1. Circuit Experiment Student Handout (Secondary Level). *Adapted from: Sellers, K., & Brackett, L. (2017) Holiday light series and parallel circuits [presentation handout]. Bureau Henry Stark Regional Office of Education 28, Atkinson, IL.*

Series and Parallel Circuits

What are Series and Parallel Circuits?

Series and parallel describes two different types of circuit arrangements. Each arrangement provides a different way for electricity to slow throughout a circuit.

❖ Series Circuits

In a series circuit, electricity has only one path on which to travel. In the example below, two bulbs are powered by a battery in a series circuit design. Electricity flows from the battery to each bulb, one at a time, in the order they are wired to the circuit. In this case, because the electricity can only flow in one path, if one of the bulbs blew out, the other bulb would not be able to light up because the flow of the electric current would have been interrupted. In the same way, if one bulb was unscrewed, the current flow to both bulbs would be interrupted.

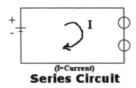

(I=Current)
Series Circuit

❖ Parallel Circuits

In a parallel circuit, electricity has more than one path on which to travel. In the example below, two bulbs are powered by a battery in a parallel circuit design. In this case, because the electricity can flow in more than one path, if one of the bulbs blew out, the other bulb would still be able to light up because the flow of electricity to the broken bulb would not stop the flow of electricity to the good bulb. In the same way, if one bulb were unscrewed, it would not prevent the other bulb from lighting up.

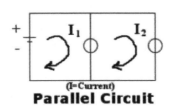

(I=Current)
Parallel Circuit

❖ What About Resistance?

The flow of electricity depends on how much resistance is in the circuit. In our examples, the bulbs provide resistance. In a series circuit, the resistance in the circuit equals the total resistance of all the bulbs. The more bulbs in the circuit the dimmer they will light. In a parallel circuit, there are multiple paths through which current can flow, so the resistance of the overall circuit is lower than it would be if only one path was available. The lower resistance means that the current will be higher and the bulbs will burn brighter compared to the same number of bulbs arranged in a series circuit.

Holiday Light Series and Parallel Circuits

❖ Instructions

You are the engineer! You need to design a system where one switch can turn on multiple lights! An example might be a string of holiday lights. Now, construct both a series circuit and a parallel circuit using aluminum foil as wires, holiday lights, 3 brass brads as the switch, tape, file folder, and a 9-Volt battery. Below is an example of a series and parallel circuit.

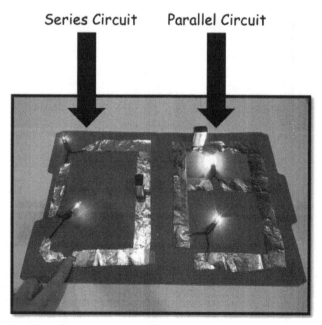

Figure 6.1.   *(continued)*

Discuss as a class how science has changed our world, how scientists have made contributions, and how African American scientists may have had to face different obstacles than white scientists in order to make their contributions to science.

Activity No. 1: Independent Reading

The students will read the book individually, either for a brief time in class or at home. As the book is read, students will keep a log of special information pertaining to each scientist. As the students read, encourage them to make note of who the author is. Also, have the students write about how they feel about the scientists at various points. How would they feel if they went through the same struggles as these scientists? If they were a scientist, what would they invent? How would the world be better with this invention? What would it take to create and implement this invention? What obstacles could they face with this invention? Would this invention receive any backlash from anyone? How realistic is the creation of this invention in today's society? What are some inventions that could help other groups and cultures?

After reading the text, the students will break into inquiry circles, choosing one or more scientists to focus on (this can be done over one or multiple class days/lessons). As the book is read, students will keep a log of special information pertaining to each scientist. The students will work together toward determining the text's main ideas, discovering cause-and-effect relationships, and making predictions and conclusions.

After you've finished and generated the list, ask students how these black scientists influenced scientists who came after them.

Activity No. 2: African American Scientists, Innovators, and Engineers "Who Am I?"

In storyboard form, the students will gather the notes and information from the book in order to outline the African American scientists that the students have studied, describing the contribution, invention, or accomplishment that each scientist made.

Based on the information from the text, students can work together toward determining the text's main ideas, discovering cause-and-effect relationships, and making predictions and conclusions in order to gain understanding on the scientists from the book.

Note: Encourage students to select and research black female scientists that were not mentioned in the book. In order to avoid gender bias, take some time to brief the students on these scientists.

Activity No. 3: Presentation

Students, working either individually, in pairs, or in groups, will select a scientist, engineer, or inventor of color to study. Students should be encouraged to research information on their individual via websites, library books, and other resources.

The students will then transfer the information to a PowerPoint presentation. On the presentation, the students should include information on who the scientist is, why they were selected, their contributions to science, the time period in which they lived and how this time period played a role in the scientist's achievements, any obstacles the scientist faced, and so on (including references).

The students will present the information to the class and teacher, and the teacher may or may not create a rubric for grading. Students can do these in each of their grade level's science classrooms/periods and have a whole-grade-level presentation on their scientists *or* students can display their scientist's information around the classroom or hallway for other class periods to see.

Activity No. 4: Interview

Students will be split into two groups, the interviewers and the scientists. Each scientist will be given an African American scientist to study and focus on, while the interviewers will create a list of questions to ask the scientists. Then, in "speed dating" style, the interviewers will rotate among the scientists and learn information about the scientists.

Activity No. 5: Electrical Circuit Stoplight

As a class, discuss Garrett A. Morgan, the inventor of the traffic light. Discuss the importance of stoplights in our world today. Ask students for predictions on how a traffic light could be made.

Prepare materials, divide students into groups, and walk students through the following steps:

1. Review the definitions of series and parallel circuits with the class. Use Figure 6.1 for background information.
2. Divide students into small groups of two to three students and distribute student worksheet and materials for each group.
3. Ask the groups to examine the schematic of a series circuit on the student worksheet and draw their own plan for series and parallel circuits in the space provided.

4. Have each group test their lights on the battery to determine the positive and negative ends of the light.
5. Have each group make a series circuit on one side of the file folder and a parallel circuit on the other side using aluminum foil for wires, three brass brads for the switch, tape, holiday lights, and a 9-volt battery. Remind students to leave a space between the wires for the switch and the battery.
6. Once the circuits are complete, ask the groups to make predictions as to how the circuits will function if the light bulb is removed. Also discuss whether the bulbs might burn brighter in one setup than another. Students should record their predictions on the student worksheet.
7. Have the groups test their predictions using their circuits, and compare their results to their predictions.
8. Bring the groups together and discuss the findings.

Extension Activity: Newspaper Publication

Using the information acquired from Activity 4 (interviews), have students work in pairs to write a newspaper-style article on the scientists they interviewed. The articles can be printed and published for the class or posted online to a classroom blog.

Tips for Struggling/Reluctant Readers

Some ways that this lesson can be differentiated for struggling or reluctant readers include, but are not limited to, tiering the assignments based on the student's level of readiness, creating interest centers/groups to motivate the students, and using flexible grouping or choice boards to select activities from a variety of learning styles.

Tips for English Language Learners/Emergent Bilinguals

Some ways that this lesson can be differentiated for English language learners include, but are not limited to, relating the content to the student's background, using and being open to a variety of types of assessment, differentiating the tasks, allowing for collaboration between students, using flexible grouping, and making the content comprehensible for all students through books or charts written in the student's first language or simplified English. These strategies allow for the English language learners to learn the same concepts as the other students in the classroom while acquiring their English language skills.

Evaluation of Skills

Tables 6.2 to 6.4 and Figure 6.1 include a student handout or teacher re-source. While these are left blank, the teacher can see a clear progression of learning for each of the objectives noted in the earlier sections of this chapter. The teacher has the flexibility to modify texts based on their students' interests, needs, and abilities.

Additional Online Resources

- American Chemical Society: www.acs.org/content/acs/en/education/resources/k-8.html
- National Education Association: www.nea.org/tools/lessons/stem-re sources.html
- Next Generation Science: www.nextgenscience.org/teachers
- Science Buddies: www.sciencebuddies.org/teacher-resources
- The National Science Foundation: www.nsf.gov/news/classroom/
- The National Science Teachers Association: www.nsta.org/publications/freebies.aspx
- UC Berkley's Understanding Science: undsci.berkeley.edu/

CONCLUDING REMARKS

Teachers should always take time to consider the populations in their classrooms, as well as their own and their student's backgrounds, cultures, viewpoints, and beliefs, as these play a major role in not only classroom environment but also student growth and understanding. Teachers should also allow for students to engage in conversations and situations that allow for them to think from another perspective outside of the one they are familiar with. For example, teachers and students alike could approach new lessons and information from a stance of getting to know others and how they have gotten to that point.

Additionally, these discussions can inspire students to examine their own lives and the lives in their community, country, and world. Furthermore, as teachers facilitate the activities and plan to assess student understanding, teachers can flexibly incorporate other science standards and objectives as needed. For example, if students have been focusing on different branches of science, such as geology, teachers can incorporate an emphasis on recognizing scientists from all backgrounds and cultures who have contributed to their discipline. This could be done through mini-activities, as well as guiding questions (such as those mentioned in the read-aloud section of the lesson) that allow the students to delve deeper into the content and examine the material from a new perspective. This can be done with the teacher in either whole group, small group, or independent formats.

REFERENCES

Blumenfeld, P. C., Soloway, E., Marx, R. W., Krajcik, J. S., Guzdial, M., & Palincsar, A. (1991). Motivating project-based learning: Sustaining the doing, supporting the learning. *Educational Psychologist, 26*(3–4), 369–398.

Chowdhary, Neelam. (2014). Global competence: A "SAGE" approach to project-based learning (deeper learning). *Teaching Channel*. Retrieved from www.teachingchannel.org/blog/2014/06/04/sage-approach-to-project-based-learning.

Haber, L. M. (1992) *Black pioneers of science and innovation*. Orlando, FL: Harcourt.

Harvey, S., & Daniels, H. (2009). *Comprehension and collaboration*. Portsmouth, NH: Heinemann.

Howard, T. C. (2012). Culturally responsive pedagogy. *Encyclopedia of Diversity in Education, 1*, 549–552.

National Research Council. (1996). *National science education standards*. Washington, DC: The National Academies Press.

Texas Education Agency (TEA). (2016). *Texas State Board for Educator Certification. English Language Arts and Reading Generalist EC–6 Standards*. Retrieved from tea.texas.gov/Texas_Educators/Preparation_and_Continuing_Education/ Approved_E%20ducator_Standards/

Tompkins, G. E. (2014). *Literacy for the 21st century: A balanced approach*. Boston, MA: Pearson.

7

Grandfather Tang's Story

A Cross-Curricular Approach Using Storytelling through Mathematics and Decision-Making Processes for Elementary Learners

Christine J. Picot

The academic and social needs of diverse populations benefit from cross-curricular learning centered on multicultural themes. These types of curricula include the learning of concepts framed within "decision making" and real-world application of concepts (Barndt, 2007). Utilizing *Grandfather Tang's Story*, students will explore the various geometric properties of two-dimensional shapes. Furthermore, exploring shape properties and constructing various figures through the use of tangrams provides students with the opportunity to work on mathematics concepts utilizing shape properties, visual/special recognition, and shape transformations.

Multicultural topics infused through the art of ancient Chinese storytelling provide the learner with the opportunity of encountering several themes to be addressed in the form of a problem scenarios. Within each grade level, these problem scenarios are addressed, highlighting themes of environmental awareness, emotions, friendship, perseverance, acceptance, and identity. These issues, in connection with utilizing geometric shape properties, provide the learner with a cross-curricular experience through a multicultural lens.

BACKGROUND OF THE LITERATURE

Grandfather Tang's Story, originally published in 1990, is written by Ann Tompert and illustrated by Robert Andrew Parker. Through the use of beautiful watercolor illustrations, Parker demonstrates impressionistic Asian tones throughout the story. Tompert cleverly integrates mathematics and culture to portray a folktale with a twist. Shape-changing traditional Chinese fox fairies and traditional Chinese tangram puzzle pieces provide the reader with scenarios of competitions as each of the fox fairies try to "outdo" one another.

The fox fairies morph into different shapes of animals using various tangram configurations. A traceable tangram is provided for the reader to engage with interactively. Through these configurations, the fox fairies learn how to address negative issues centered on *pride*. Furthermore, themes of grandparents, culture, identity, and friendship are woven throughout the story.

These themes facilitate questions as catalysts for stimulating conversations centered on community building through themes of perseverance, acceptance, and identity. It is through these themes and the use of tangrams that the students will create their own stories based on decision-making processes and scenarios.

PEDAGOGICAL APPROACH

The 21st Century Learning Standards are acknowledged though learning projects focusing on the ability for students to develop thinking skills, content knowledge, and social and emotional competencies through social and cross-cultural skills learning (Moylan, 2008). The academic and social needs of diverse populations benefit from cross-curricular learning centered on multicultural themes.

These types of curricula include the learning of concepts framed within "decision making" and real-world application of concepts (Barndt, 2007). Through the lens of ancient Chinese storytelling and puzzle pieces, these lessons provide students with the ability to explore solution options to problem scenarios using creative writing in mathematics.

Writing in mathematics provides assessment, social, and cognitive benefits. For example, Aspinwall and Aspinwall (2003) note that writing provided teachers with a window into students' perceptions and knowledge that was essential for planning purposeful instruction. Similarly, Vygotsky (1962) noted that writing makes a unique demand in that the writer must engage in "deliberate structuring of the web of meaning" (p. 100).

From a social perspective, writing has the potential to facilitate communication. For example, Englert, Mariage, and Dunsmore (2006) noted the importance of Vygotsky (1978) and Bahktin's (1986) views of the social implication of writing by referencing the following statements: "Higher psychological processes, such as writing and reading, have their origins in social processes that occur on an interpsychological plane, and that are mediated through language signs, symbols, actions and objects" (Vygotsky, 1978, p. 208).

Within the field of mathematics, there are four types of mathematics writing prompts. These types of prompts are (1) content, (2) process, (3) affective, and (4) narrative prompts (Baxter, Woodward, & Olsen, 2005; Dougherty, 1996; Shield & Galbraith, 1998; Urquhart, 2009). A *content* prompt, according to Urquhart (2009), is one that attends to mathematical concepts and relationships. Student responses can be in the form of defining, comparing and contrasting, and explaining.

A *process* type of prompt invoked student responses regarding the selection of the various strategies, or the steps used to solve a process problem (Dougherty, 1996). An *affective prompt* requires students to construct an answer that is associated with an attitude or feeling about mathematics. According to Dougherty (1996), these types of prompts provide a more holistic view of how students view mathematics.

The *narrative* prompt is a type of journal writing prompt. These types of prompts are commonly used for purposes of high-stakes testing. Within this type of prompt, the constructed response can be in the form of a response that portrays math content in an imaginary or real-world sense. Furthermore, mathematical *narrative* content and themes are embedded within children's literature (Burns, 2004; Whitin & Whitin, 2000).

The research types of writing mathematics textbooks offer are limited in the amount of narrative prompts (Joseph, 2012). It is therefore up to the teacher to create and develop these types to supplement the cross-curricular instruction.

Similar to reading acquisition, these narrative prompts can be thought of as facilitating unconstrained skills, whereby the student is provided the opportunity to connect the mathematics content to real-world application or narrative element (versus strictly computation). According to Dougherty Stahl (2011), assessing isolated skills reflects mastery of constrained abilities rather than making sense of texts or unconstrained abilities.

Multicultural Education

Multicultural education is embedded within various methods of instruction such as project-based learning (Voronchenko, Klimenko, & Kostina, 2015; Chakrabarty & Muhamed, 2013). The common thread within these types of lessons is a focus on inquiry-based learning through problem scenarios utilizing geometric conceptual understanding.

Within this vein, national standards are addressed within social studies, health, and English language arts (NCSS, 2010; NHES, 2007; IRA/NCTE, 1996). These lessons include topics of how the study of individual development and identity will help students to describe factors important to the development of personal identity. Students will have discussions centered on personal identities in the context of families, peers, schools, and communities (NCSS, 2010).

Health standards (NHES, 2007) can also be acknowledged whereby students will have discussions centered on health-related situations that might require a thoughtful decision. Analyze when assistance is needed in making a health-related decision. List healthy options to health-related issues or problems and predict the potential outcomes of each option when making a health-related decision in each of the problem scenarios.

These lessons also have elements encompassed within the English language arts/reading standards (IRA/NCTE, 1996) to include engaging effectively in a range of collaborative discussions (one-on-one, in groups, and teacher-led) with diverse partners on *topics and texts*, building on others' ideas and expressing their own clearly.

Furthermore, students will write opinion/persuasive letters on topics or texts, supporting a point of view with reasons. With guidance and support from adults, they will produce writing in which the development and organization are appropriate to task and purpose. Students will recount stories, including fables, folktales, and myths from diverse cultures; determine the central message, lesson, or moral; and explain how it is conveyed through key details in the text. Students will also determine a theme of a story, drama, or poem from details in the text, including how characters in a story or drama respond to challenges.

The lessons created for this chapter highlight this feature of problem solving through the use of mathematical writing and decision making focusing on standards of mathematics. Furthermore, elements of social studies, health, and English language arts/reading standards in K–5 learning are also present.

Lesson Objectives

Each of the lessons within this chapter align to each of the standards mentioned below in the content area of mathematics with a focus on geometry. Standards and topics within social studies, health, and English language arts/reading are embedded throughout each of the grade-level lesson plan objectives.

Mathematics

National Council of Teachers of Mathematics *Principles and Standards for School Mathematics* (NTCM, 2000)

Analyze characteristics and properties of two- and three-dimensional geometric shapes and develop mathematical arguments about geometric relationships.

Pre-K–2 Expectations: In pre-K through grade 2 each and every student should:

- recognize, name, build, draw, compare, and sort two- and three-dimensional shapes;
- describe attributes and parts of two- and three-dimensional shapes; and
- investigate and predict the results of putting together and taking apart two- and three-dimensional shapes.

Grades 3–5 Expectations: In grades 3–5 each and every student should:

- identify, compare, and analyze attributes of two- and three-dimensional shapes and develop vocabulary to describe the attributes;
- classify two- and three-dimensional shapes according to their properties and develop definitions of classes of shapes such as triangles and pyramids;
- investigate, describe, and reason about the results of subdividing, combining, and transforming shapes;
- explore congruence and similarity; and
- make and test conjectures about geometric properties and relationships and develop logical arguments to justify conclusions.

Apply transformations and use symmetry to analyze mathematical situations.

Pre-K–2 Expectations: In pre-K through grade 2 each and every student should:

- recognize and apply slides, flips, and turns; and
- recognize and create shapes that have symmetry.

Grades 3–5 Expectations: In grades 3–5 each and every student should:

- predict and describe the results of sliding, flipping, and turning two-dimensional shapes;
- describe a motion or a series of motions that will show that two shapes are congruent; and

- identify and describe line and rotational symmetry in two- and three-dimensional shapes and designs.

Use visualization, spatial reasoning, and geometric modeling to solve problems.

Pre–K–2 Expectations: In pre-K through grade 2 each and every student should:

- create mental images of geometric shapes using spatial memory and spatial visualization;
- recognize and represent shapes from different perspectives;
- relate ideas in geometry to ideas in number and measurement; and
- recognize geometric shapes and structures in the environment and specify their location.

Grades 3–5 Expectations: In grades 3–5 each and every student should:

- build and draw geometric objects;
- create and describe mental images of objects, patterns, and paths;
- identify and build a three-dimensional object from two-dimensional representations of that object;
- identify and draw a two-dimensional representation of a three-dimensional object;
- use geometric models to solve problems in other areas of mathematics, such as number and measurement; and
- recognize geometric ideas and relationships and apply them to other disciplines and to problems that arise in the classroom or in everyday life.

Content Overview

In this lesson, students will encounter a problem situation posed in a letter format from the characters in the story (Grandfather or the fox fairies). Depending on the grade level, students will use decision making and collaborative efforts to address problem scenarios while creating a storytelling solution.

These problem scenarios will require the students to use tangram pieces to develop their stories (just like Grandfather) to illustrate the content within. The problem scenarios will be related to multicultural themes and posed in the format of writing prompts highlighting the themes of perseverance, acceptance, and identity.

The writing prompts may be interchangeable and utilized with all grade levels (although each grade level has a specific prompt) depending on topic focus. The prompts may also be modified to meet the literacy needs of your learners. Each grade-level prompt will have a different letter related to issues addressing themes related to multiculturalism. The planning template provides teacher flexibility in composition for Steps 1–4:

- Step 1 and Step 2: Required to build background knowledge related to the components within the story, such as storytelling and tangrams. The questions may be modified to include further probing questions and sub-questions.
- Step 3: The problem-solving letter written to the students. All students in the group should have a copy of the letter for active reading.
- Step 4: Planning outline for students (in groups) to draft their story addressing the problem topic (multicultural) utilizing the tangram pieces.
- Step 5: Possible student solutions in a letter writing format. Possible student solutions and writing rubric are located in the "Evaluation of Skills" section below.

Furthermore, the stories can be drafted individually or as one group submission. Copies of the resources needed are provided in the "Additional Resources" section.

Materials/Supplies

- Tompert, A., & Parker, R. A. (1990). *Grandfather Tang's story*. New York: Crown Publishers.
- Lesson planning template
- Copies of tangram pieces
- Copies of tangram animals
- Tangram videos and background building questions
- Copies of blank paper for drafting decisions

SEQUENCE OF ACTIVITIES

Each of the following sections are utilized for each of the grade levels indicated. The sections have samples of questions and prompts designed to be used flexibly throughout the lesson plan. Each grade level has a different story problem unique to the theme of the level of students. Example tangram pieces in section 5 provide the learner with options for illustrating the story they have completed during the collaborative decision-making processes for the solution to the problem.

Step No. 1: Read-Aloud

During the read-aloud and based on grade-level expectations, teachers will build background knowledge related to ancient Chinese storytelling by addressing the following guiding questions (not limited to):

- What is storytelling?
- Do you have grandparents?
- Have your grandparents ever told you a story about traditions?
- Why is storytelling useful in culture building?
- Why are fox-fairies used in this Chinese storytelling?
- Can you think of other animals used in fables or folktales for storytelling?
- Why are tangrams used in this storytelling?
- Can you think of other stories that are told to solve problems? The Tortoise and the Hare?

Step No. 2: Exploring Tangram Pieces

Based on grade-level expectations, teachers will build background knowledge related to the ancient Chinese puzzle tangrams by addressing the following guiding questions (not limited to):

- How many pieces are in the tangram puzzle?
- What are the shapes?
- What are the sizes?
- What are the names of the shapes?
- Are there any rules when making figures using all seven tangram pieces?
- Can you make a square, triangle, rectangle?

Further background knowledge in the form of question sheets and videos about tangrams are found below in the "Additional Resources" section.

Step 3: Grandfather Tang's Letters

Kindergarten Prompt—Theme: Environmental Awareness
Dear Students,
I have a problem and I need your help. Fox Fairy 1 and Fox Fairy 2 are running around the neighborhood leaving trash everywhere they go. If they

have food wrappers or a drink cup, they throw it on the ground! The turtle and the fish also said they are having a hard time swimming because they are throwing their trash into the water where they live!

I am very sad and need your help figuring out how I can help these two Fox Fairies understand the importance of keeping our environment clean. Why is it important to keep our environment clean? What happens if you don't keep our environment clean?

If you would talk about these problems and then write or draw a picture to answer these questions that would be very helpful. I will give your drawings and sentences to the Fox Fairies so that they can learn how to do things differently to help our environment.

P.S.: You could also let the Fox Fairies know what you do in your classroom, school, and neighborhood to help keep the environment clean.

I look forward to looking at your drawings and reading your sentences to the Fox Fairies so we can help them make good choices.
Thank you,
Grandfather Tang

First Grade Prompt—Theme: Emotions
Dear Students,

I have a problem and I need your help. Fox Fairy 1 is having a problem crying when he doesn't get his way. He will cry when he has a problem with his brother, Fox Fairy 2. He will cry when his grandmother says he can't have something he wants. His teacher also said he cries in school when he has conflicts with some of his friends (turtle, fish, lion). It seems like when Fox Fairy 1 gets angry or frustrated, he cries.

This makes me very worried because I want Fox Fairy 1 to be able to control his feelings and emotions. When Fox Fairy 1 has a problem at home or at school, what could he do instead of getting upset and crying? What do you do when you are upset or frustrated? Could you please draft a letter with a few sentences and a picture of some ideas you have that can help Fox Fairy control his emotions?

I look forward to looking at your drawings and reading your sentences to Fox Fairy 1 so we can help him learn how to control his emotions.
Thank you,
Grandfather Tang

Second Grade Prompt—Theme: Friendship
Dear Students,

I have a problem and I need your help. Fox Fairy 1 and the Dog decided to race each other one day. The Dog won the race, which made Fox Fairy 1 very upset. Fox Fairy 1 is so upset that he does not want to be friends with the Dog any longer. The Dog has tried to be nice to Fox Fairy 1 by saving him a seat in lunch, trying to make him laugh, even trying to help him with his homework. However, Fox Fairy 1 just ignores him and walks away.

Have you and your best friend ever argued about something? Why is it important to talk about your feelings? What ideas do you have for Fox Fairy 1 and the Dog in order to be friends again? Could you please draft a short letter to Fox Fairy 1 and Dog about how they can solve this problem?

I look forward to looking at your drawings and reading your sentences to the Fox Fairy 1 and the Dog so we can help their friendship.
Thank you,
Grandfather Tang

Third Grade Prompt—Theme: Perseverance
Dear Students,

I have a problem and I need your help. Fox Fairy 1 has turned into a rabbit and Fox Fairy 2 has turned into a turtle. Both Fox Fairies have decided to enter a race. However, Fox Fairy 2 (the turtle) doesn't feel like he should compete in the race because he thinks he will lose. He is worried that he is not fast enough and wants to quit. Could you please draft a story to Fox Fairy 2 about why it's important to not quit and whether or not you think it's important to win all the time?

I look forward to reading your stories to Fox Fairy 2. We want to motivate Fox Fairy 2 to do his best and not quit.
Thank you,
Grandfather Tang

Fourth Grade Prompt—Theme: Acceptance
Dear Students,

I have a problem and I need your help. Fox Fairy 1 is making fun of Fox Fairy 2 because he has different color fur from him. Fox Fairy 2 has changed into different animals (turtle, lion, squirrel) so that Fox Fairy 1 will accept him. However, it is not working. How can I help communicate to Fox Fairy 1 that Fox Fairy 2 has great qualities beyond the color of his fur coat? Could you please draft a story to Fox Fairy 1 about why it's important to understand the idiom "not to judge a book by the cover"?

I look forward to reading your stories to Fox Fairy 1. We want to motivate Fox Fairy 1 to accept and respect all Fox Fairies even if they look different.
Thank you,
Grandfather Tang

Fifth Grade Prompt—Theme: Identity

Dear Students,

I have a problem and I need your help. Fox Fairy 1 is feeling a little down lately. He wants to be another animal, one who is faster and stronger and more beautiful. I have given Fox Fairy 1 the power to shape-shift into any animal he wants (hawk, lion, fish). However, I am not sure I made the right decision in giving him this choice. I want him to be happy with who he is.

Can you please help me to draft a letter of what animal you think Fox Fairy 1 should be if he could change? Or perhaps he should stay the same? I am not sure and need your help drafting a story you think might help him to accept who he is, even if he changes, and why you feel he will be happier with the change or staying the same.

I look forward to reading your stories to Fox Fairy 1. We want to motivate Fox Fairy 1 to find joy in his abilities and appearance.

Thank you,

Grandfather Tang

Step No. 4: Addressing the Problem

Engage students in a class discussion of the problem posed by Grandfather Tang. Ask students:

- What is the problem?
- How can we solve the problem? What advice can we give?
- What are the steps taken to solve the problem?
- Why is this a good solution?

Step No. 5: Letter to Grandfather Tang

Students draft a mini-story to send to Grandfather Tang about their solutions to the problem. They use the tangram pieces to illustrate their stories.

Tips for Struggling Readers

There are various ways this lesson can be differentiated: tiering the vocabulary and language within the problem prompt to meet the student's needs; providing a template for drafting the letter to scaffold the process of composition; incorporating technology such as Microsoft Word, PowerPoint, or various Whiteboard applications (ShowMe: www.showme.com), for drafting and editing along with peer-reviewing processes. This may enhance the instruction for the final draft.

Tips for English Language Learners

Build background knowledge of tangram pieces and the mathematical attributes. Focus on cultural components of storytelling from various ethnicities. Feature mini-lessons encompassing language structures such as idioms, central message, and themes and the moral of the story.

Evaluation of Skills

The following showcases examples of student affordances at each grade level. A general rubric is designed to provide flexible options for assessing student writing at each grade level.

Kindergarten Possible Solutions/Extension

A document/letter should be drafted to Grandfather highlighting student solutions to encompass what it means to keep our environment clean by discussing each question as a class: *Why is it important to keep our environment clean? What happens if you don't keep our environment clean?*

Students can work in groups on chart paper or individual writing paper to draft a statement or an illustration with labels to Grandfather highlighting the answers to the question/s with a focus on environmental awareness. Topics of discussion may include implications of littering on land and in our oceans, recycling, animal and sea life, and how transfer of learning can impact our classroom area and school environment. Sample tangram illustrations include the fox fairies, turtle, and fish.

Hands-on projects can include service to the school by campus walk cleanup.

Grade 1 Possible Solutions

A document/letter should be drafted to Grandfather highlighting student solutions to encompass what it means to control our emotions by discussing each question as a class: *When Fox Fairy 1 has a problem at home or at school, what could he do instead of getting upset and crying? What do you do when you are upset or frustrated? Could you please draft a letter with a few sentences and a picture of some ideas you have that can help Fox Fairy control his emotions?*

Students can then work in groups on chart paper or individual writing paper to draft a statement with an illustration to Grandfather highlighting the answers to the question/s with a focus on how to control emotions when faced with a challenge. Topics of discussion may include how to talk about situations when you are upset and words to communicate feelings to include "I Statements." Sample tangram illustrations include the fox fairy, turtle, fish, and/or lion.

Grade 2 Possible Solutions

A document/letter should be drafted to Grandfather highlighting student solutions to encompass what it means to be a friend by discussing each question as a class: *Have you and your best friend ever argued about something? Why is it important to talk about your feelings? What ideas do you have for Fox Fairy 1 and the Dog in order to be friends again?*

Students can then work in groups on chart paper or individual writing paper to draft a statement with a tangram illustration to Grandfather highlighting the answers to the question/s with a focus on what friendship means. Topics of discussion may include what it "looks like" to be a friend. Discussions regarding competitive events—winning vs. losing—can also be included. Sample tangram illustrations include the fox fairy and the dog.

Grade 3 Possible Solutions

A letter should be drafted to Grandfather highlighting student solutions to encompass what it means to persevere even when you feel like quitting by addressing/discussing topic questions (with the whole class or in small groups) in the letter to include: *Insecurities about losing the race. Issues of the consequences of quitting. Could you please draft a story to Fox Fairy 2 about why it's important to not quit and whether or not you think it's important to win all the time?*

Students can then work in groups on chart paper or individual writing paper to draft a statement with a tangram illustration to Grandfather highlighting the answers to the question/s with a focus on perseverance. Sample tangram illustrations include the fox fairies and a turtle.

Grade 4 Possible Solutions

A letter should be drafted to grandfather highlighting student solutions to encompass what it means to have an attitude of acceptance by addressing/discussing topic questions (with the whole class or in small groups) in the letter to include: *How can I help communicate to Fox Fairy 1 that Fox Fairy 2 has great qualities beyond the color of his fur coat? Importance of understanding the meaning behind the idiom "not to judge a book by the cover."*

Students can then work in groups on chart paper or individual writing paper to draft a letter with a tangram illustration to Grandfather highlighting the answers to the question/s with a focus on acceptance. Sample tangram illustrations include various tangram animals (turtle, lion, squirrel) and the fox fairies.

Grade 5 Possible Solutions

A letter should be drafted to grandfather highlighting student solutions to encompass what it means to reflect on and accept who you are and the changes that you want to make in order to reach your identity goals by addressing/discussing topic questions (with the whole class or in small groups) in the letter to include: *Should you change your identity based on other's opinions? Consequences of conforming? Not conforming? Accepting who you are. Ability to make positive changes.*

Students can then work in groups on chart paper or individual writing paper to draft a letter with a tangram illustration to Grandfather highlighting the answers to the question/s with a focus on identity. Sample tangram illustrations include various tangram animals (hawk, lion, fish) and the fox fairy.

Additional Resources

- Tangram: https://www.thoughtco.com/tangrams-geometry-worksheet-2312325
- Tangram Animals: http://www.auntannie.com/Geometric/Tangrams/PuzzleSheets/TangAnimalsClr.pdf
- Tangram Videos and Background Building Questions: https://www.thoughtco.com/tangrams-geometry-worksheet-2312325

CONCLUDING REMARKS

Making sense of mathematics through the lens of literature can assist students in making connections across the curriculum. Listening, speaking, reading, and writing are infused within the various multicultural topics and themes addressed in the story plot. Furthermore, mathematical vocabulary through geometric concepts are utilized in drafting responses within the various modalities of learning.

Students can begin to acquire the language needed to become mathematically literate while focusing on decision-making and problem-solving scenarios. Using themes within multicultural education in the K–5 classroom while connecting to mathematics topics can benefit students in making real-world connections to controversial topics that may otherwise be uncomfortable to address—or be avoided altogether.

The letter writing in this chapter, according to grade-level topics, provides the venue for addressing issues that students may encounter in their daily lives. Learning how to address these topics within the early grade levels can provide the interventions needed related to multicultural issues as they progress through the elementary grade levels in order to become culturally literate and responsive citizens.

REFERENCES

Aspinwall, L., & Aspinwall, J. (2003). Investigating mathematical thinking using open writing prompts. *Mathematics Teaching in the Middle School, 8*(7), 350–353.

Bakhtin, M. (1986). The problem of text in linguistics, philology, and the human sciences: An experiment in philosophical analysis. In M. M. Bakhtin, *Speech genres and other late essays* (pp. 103–131). Austin: University of Texas Press.

Baxter, J. A., Woodward, J., & Olson, D. (2005). Writing in mathematics: An alternative form of communication for academically low-achieving students. *Learning Disabilities Research & Practice, 20*(2), 119–135.

Brandt, J. (2007). *Understanding and dismantling racism: The twenty-first century challenge to white America.* Minneapolis, MN: Fortress Press.

Burns, M. (2004). Writing in math. *Educational Leadership, 10*, 30–33.

Chakrabarty, S., & Muhamed, N. (2013). Problem based learning: Cultural diverse students' engagement, learning and contextualized problem solving in a mathematics class. *WCIK E-Journal of Integration Knowledge*, 38–49.

Dougherty, B. (1996). The write way: A look at journal writing in first-year algebra. *The Mathematics Teacher, 89*(7), 556–560.

Dougherty Stahl, K. A. (2011). Applying new visions of reading development in today's classrooms. *The Reading Teacher: A Journal of Research-Based Classroom Practice, 65*(1), 52–56. doi: 10.1598/RT.65.1.7.

Englert, S., Mariage, T. V., & Dunsmore, K. (2006). Tenets of sociocultural theory in writing instruction research. In C. A. MacArthur, S. Graham, & J. Fitzgerald (Eds.), *Handbook of writing research* (pp. 208–221). New York: Guilford Press.

Health of Children. (2012). Multicultural education & curriculum. Retrieved from http://www.healthofchildren.com/M/Multicultural-Education-Curriculum.html

ILA NCTE. (2019). ReadWriteThink.org. Retrieved from http://www.readwritethink.org

International Reading Association and the National Council of Teachers of English. (1996). *Standards for the English language arts.* Newark, DE: IRA/NCTE.

Joint Committee on National Health Education Standards. (2007). *National health education standards: Achieving excellence* (2nd ed.). Atlanta, GA: American Cancer Society.

Joseph, C. M. (2012). Communication and academic vocabulary in mathematics: A content analysis of prompts eliciting written responses in two elementary mathematics textbooks. University of South Florida, Tampa, FL. ProQuest Digital Dissertations. UMI: 3547434.

Moylan, W. A. (2008). Learning by project: Developing essential 21st century skills using student team projects. *International Journal, 15*(9).

National Council for the Social Studies. (2010). *National curriculum standards for social studies: A framework for teaching, learning, and assessment.* Silver Spring, MD: NCSS.

National Council of Teachers of Mathematics. (2000). *Principles and standards for school mathematics.* Reston, VA: NCTM.

Russel, Deb. (2017, August 21). ThoughtCo. What are tangrams. Retrieved from https://www.thoughtco.com/tangrams-geometry-worksheet-2312325

Shield, M., & Galbraith, P. (1998). The analysis of student expository writing in mathematics. *Educational Studies in Mathematics, 36*(1), 29–52.

Tompert, A., & Parker, R. A. (1990). *Grandfather Tang's story.* New York: Crown Publishers.

Voronchenko, T., Klimenko, T., & Kostina, I., (2015). Learning to live in a global world: Project-based learning in multicultural student groups as a pedagogy of tolerance strategy. *Procedia—Social and Behavioral Sciences, 191*, 1489–1495. Retrieved from http://linkinghub.elsevier.com/retrieve/pii/S1877042815027329

Urquhart, V. (2009). *Using Writing in Mathematics to Deepen Student Learning.* Retrieved from the Mid-continent Research for Education and Learning (McCREL) at https://files.eric.ed.gov/fulltext/ED544239.pdf

Urquhart, V., & McIver, M. (2005). *Teaching writing in the content areas.* Alexandria, VA: Association for Supervision and Curriculum Development (ASCD).

Vygotsky, L. S. (1962). *Thought and language.* Cambridge, MA: MIT Press.

Vygotsky, L. S. (1978). *Mind in society: The development of higher psychological processes.* Cambridge, MA: Harvard University Press.

Whitin, D., & Whitin, P. (2000). Exploring mathematics through talking and writing. In M. J. Burke & F. R. Curcio (Eds.), *Learning mathematics for a new century*, (pp. 213–222). Reston, VA: National Council of Teachers of Mathematics.

8

Ruth and the Green Book

Using Mathematics to Better Understand Discrimination

Amy K. Corp

This chapter utilizes problem-based learning to connect mathematics to understanding the depths of injustice during the Jim Crow era. The story *Ruth and the Green Book* recounts the fictional character of Ruth on a journey from Chicago to visit her grandmother in Birmingham, Alabama. The story provides a historically accurate portrayal of Jim Crow from her perspective as an African American youngster.

Lessons in this chapter require students to put themselves in the father's place and solve the problem of traveling from North to South without racist incidents. Students are given 1960s parameters for travel and a copy of *The Negro Motorist Green Book* (*The Green Book*) to locate friendly places to stop. As students plot these routes on a map and discuss the differences, in time and distance, to the shortest route, they cultivate a deeper understanding of how racism negatively impacted the family's travel.

BACKGROUND OF THE LITERATURE

Ruth and her parents travel from Chicago to Alabama during the era of Jim Crow to visit her grandmother. Readers follow Ruth's journey to the southern state as her parents use the advice of *The Green Book* (a book of friendly places for African Americans). Her story recounts the prejudice and kindness they experienced along the way.

Illustrations by Floyd Cooper are affirming and authentic to the era and culture. The text is realistic as told through the eyes of a child and encourages the reader to emotionally experience how it feels to encounter racism.

This fictional story gives a personal account of what Ruth experienced, and children will identify and/or empathize with her emotions and reactions to being treated unjustly.

PEDAGOGICAL APPROACH

This chapter utilizes an integration approach to combine mathematics and reading. The story presents students with the problem that many African Americans faced during the era of Jim Crow: how to travel safely to avoid discrimination. Implementing problem-based learning, students use their mathematical skills to determine plausible routes based on *The Green Book* for friendly stops.

Through mathematical reasoning and problem solving, students determine that the trip took longer, was farther, and was more expensive. As a result, students have strong evidence to conclude that Jim Crow laws were purposefully created to discriminate against African American people.

This type of problem-based learning becomes powerful as it empowers students to better understand circumstances within a story (Moyer, 2000). In this case, the problem-based learning is meaningful because students see from Ruth's encounter with Jim Crow how these rules were created and used to make African Americans feel inferior and unwelcome (the root of racism).

One goal of this lesson is to create space to discuss an outcome of racism/prejudice by learning how the route changed due to Jim Crow laws. Previous discussions of the book (during the initial reading of the story) lead to a better understanding of what racism is, how to identify it then and perhaps connect to it now, and how to build empathy for those who experienced and still experience racism.

Incorporating mathematics helps students better understand how the characters were impacted by racism. Instead of just reading about their journey south, students have to use mathematics to solve the problem of traveling the most cautious route and can mathematically describe the extra time, distance, and expense this involved. By choosing a narrative that does not highlight the dominant culture but features the "other" perspective (especially in mixed but mostly white classrooms), students of color are less marginalized and are more empowered to engage (Delpit, 2012).

By utilizing a picture book, all students should be able to better identify with how discrimination feels and reflect on their own actions with others. Students connect to stories that represent their culture and naturally are more engaged with activities that follow (Corp, 2017; Iliev & D'Angelo, 2014).

After an initial discussion of the story, students connect to the mathematics through a problem-based learning approach that Ruth's father must have utilized in order to travel safely from their home to Grandma's. Students utilize problem-solving strategies and engage in practicing mathematical concepts (like addition, subtraction, estimation, elapsed time, multiplication, and division).

After students understand the problems of traveling during Jim Crow as African Americans and how mathematics is the vehicle for a solution, they work in groups to determine a plausible safe route for the trip south or for the return trip.

Students will also integrate geographic skills such as map reading and direction as they use their copy of *The Green Book* for locations to stop along their devised route. Students may also incorporate technology by using Google Maps to calculate distances between possible stops on their determined routes.

Lesson Objectives

NCTM Process Standards

- Problem solving:
  - The student will build new mathematical knowledge through problem solving.
  - The student will solve problems that arise in mathematics and in other contexts.
  - The student will apply and adapt a variety of appropriate strategies to solve problems.
- Communication:
  - The student will organize and consolidate their mathematical thinking through communication.
  - The student will communicate their mathematical thinking coherently and clearly to peers, teachers, and others.
  - The student will analyze and evaluate the mathematical thinking and strategies of others.
  - The student will use the language of mathematics to express mathematical ideas precisely.
- Connections:
  - The student will recognize and use connections among mathematical ideas.
  - The student will understand how mathematical ideas interconnect and build on one another to produce a coherent whole.

- ○ The student will recognize and apply mathematics in contexts outside of mathematics.
- • Representations:
  - ○ The student will select, apply, and translate among mathematical representations to solve problems.
  - ○ The student will use representations to model and interpret physical, social, and mathematical phenomena.

NCTM Content Standards That May Be Incorporated:

- • Pre-K–2:
  - ○ The student will connect number words and numerals to the quantities they represent, using various physical models and representations.
  - ○ The student will understand the effects of adding and subtracting whole numbers.
  - ○ The student will use a variety of methods and tools to compute, including objects, mental computation, and estimation.
  - ○ The student will recognize the attribute of time.
- • 3–5:
  - ○ The student will understand the effects of multiplying and dividing whole numbers.
  - ○ The student will identify and use relationships between operations, such as division as the inverse of multiplication, to solve problems.
  - ○ The student will develop and use strategies to estimate the results of whole-number computations and to judge the reasonableness of such results.
  - ○ The student will understand and calculate elapsed time.
- • 6–8:
  - ○ The student will understand and use the inverse relationships of addition and subtraction, multiplication and division to simplify computations and solve problems.
- • 9–12
  - ○ The students will make decisions about units and scales that are appropriate for problem situations involving measurement.

Content Overview

In this lesson, students across all grade levels will identify, through problem-based learning, the injustices of Jim Crow laws and the ingenuity and creative collaboration of African Americans to devise their own network of safe places for fuel, groceries, and lodging while traveling in hostile areas. Students will identify the problem in the story and identify the mathematical skills needed to help them plan stops appropriate for safe travel to or from Alabama.

Then, with a small group or partner, students will devise a plausible route (or return route) for a safe trip. Students will share the information they have learned using maps, drawings, tables, and oral presentations, depending on what is appropriate for the students and grade level. Mathematical and operational skills could include elapsed time, estimation, comparing numbers into the thousands, multiplication, division, creating tables with estimations of time and distance, using scale, and rate of change.

Materials/Supplies

- Ramsey, C., & Strauss, G. (2010). *Ruth and the Green Book*. Minneapolis, MN: Carolrhoda Books.
- Computers or devices with Internet access to Google Maps or printed maps
- Copies of *The Green Book* (or pdf: http://www.autolife.umd.umich.edu/Race/R_Casestudy/87_135_1736_GreenBk.pdf)
- Notebooks and paper
- Rulers to work with map scale (if using printed maps)
- Writing utensils
- Poster board, scissors, glue

SEQUENCE OF ACTIVITIES

Elementary

Hook

Share with the class a memory of going on a road trip. Invite them to share their experiences. Ask if along their way anyone treated them rudely or asked them to leave. Then tell them that in today's lesson they're going to see how people were treated unjustly based on their skin color and how they relied on mathematics to make their trip better.

Activity No. 1: Read-Aloud

The teacher will read *Ruth and the Green Book*. At appropriate times during the reading, ask, "How would that make you feel?" After reading ask students to reflect on these questions (aloud or in small groups): Why couldn't Ruth's family just take the fastest route? Why did they purchase a

Green Book? What was this book about? How and why did this change their possible route? What mathematics did Daddy use to get them safely to Alabama? Encourage them to think about time and distance. You may want to write some of these connections on the board.

Activity No. 2: Creating a Plan

Thinking back to the hook, ask students, "Today when you want to travel, how do you (or your parents) plan when and where to stop?" Discuss and then explain their task. Students work in pairs or groups of four to determine a plausible route that Ruth's family traveled according to clues from the story and Google Maps.

The route is likely through Indiana, Kentucky (rolling hills, Jim Crow rules at the restroom), and Tennessee. Assign Birmingham as Grandma's town. Students use the directions feature on Google Maps and a copy of the Green Book (www.autolife.umd.umich.edu/Race/R_Casestudy/Negro_mo torist_green_bk.htm) to plot out the cities along the route that they determine as plausible.

Students must consider these parameters: when to get gas (tank=210 miles, the 1952 Buick gets 16 miles per gallon), the speed limit at the time was 55 mph on main roads, and the most Daddy wanted to drive during the day was 9 hours.

Activity No. 3: Representation

Students, working in pairs or in groups, review their route for reasonableness (they aren't driving too far, they aren't stopping too late, and they have

Table 8.1.   Creating a Plan Example

Day	Driving Times and Stops	Distance
Day 1: Chicago to Lafayette, IN	Drive about 2 hours to Lafayette, IN. Get gas at Essl, eat at Pekin Café on Hartford Street (30 min.).	125 miles
Lafayette, IN to Louisville, KY	Drive about 3 hours to Louisville, KY. Get gas at F&M service station on Walnut Street (time to stretch and use restrooms there, 30 min.).	176 miles
Louisville, KY to Nashville, TN	Drive about 3 hours to Nashville, TN. Stay at Carver Courts Hotel on White Creek's Pike.	180
Totals for this day:	8 hours driving and 1 hour in breaks = 9 hours.	481 miles (about 500 miles)

enough gas to get to each stop). The students will then transfer the information to a printed (or group-created) map with marked cities and a timetable or chart to show their stops for gas, food, and lodging and present or display them to the class.

Activity No. 4: Challenge

Students work (in same groups, pairs, or individually) to create a plan for a different safe return route for Ruth and her parents using the Green Book and Google Maps. To challenge students, remind them that on the return trip they likely only had breakfast and lunch with them from Grandma, so they need to plan food stops also. Students create a table for time and distance traveled each day. Students display their thinking in a chart with friendly stops, time, and/or miles and by marking the route on a printed map. Encourage students to explain verbally or in writing why they chose this route.

Middle

Hook

Share with the class a personal memory of going on a road trip. Invite them to briefly share their experiences. Ask if while stopping along their journey anyone treated them rudely or asked them to leave. Then tell them that in today's lesson they are going to see how people were treated unjustly and how they utilized mathematics to make their trip better.

Activity No. 1: Read-Aloud

The teacher will read *Ruth and the Green Book*. After reading ask students to reflect on these questions (aloud or in small groups): Why couldn't Ruth's family just take the fastest route? How would being barred from using the restroom or staying in a place make you feel? What was *The Green Book* and why did they buy one? How and why did this change their possible route? What mathematics did her father use to get them safely to Alabama? You may want to write some of these connections on the board.

Activity No. 2: Creating a Plan

Thinking back to the hook, ask students, "Today, when you want to travel, how do you (or your parents) plan when and where to stop?" Since most will answer with technology, let students know they will use the directions feature at Google Maps and a copy of the Green Book (www.autolife.umd.umich.

edu/Race/R_Casestudy/Negro_motorist_green_bk.htm) to plot out the cities along the route that they determine as part of a plausible route back from Birmingham to Chicago, in partners or groups of four.

Students must consider these parameters (also provided in the resources): when to get gas (tank=210 miles, the 1952 Buick gets 16 miles per gallon, and the speed limit at the time was 55 mph on main roads), where to eat and duration of stop, and that they would only drive 9 hours a day. Students plot the rate of travel for each day or graph to demonstrate the distance traveled over time each day. They should also total the time and distance for the trip (see Table 8.1).

Activity No. 3: Representation

Students, working in pairs or in groups, review their route for reasonableness (they aren't driving too far, they aren't stopping too late, and they have enough gas to get to each stop). The students will then transfer the information to a printed map with labeled stops and a timetable or chart to show their stops for gas, food, and lodging and their graph for distance traveled over time.

Students could present these to the class or create a short video explaining their route with details from their timetable or chart(s) for the teacher to view or share as appropriate. You could challenge students to add a scale to their map and make their stops accurate to the scale. The teacher may want to create a rubric for grading including reasoning, computation skills, and data presentation (see Table 8.2).

Activity No. 4: Challenge

Students should research and compare the cost of the route designed to avoid discrimination and racist encounters to the cost of the fastest route (see resources for link to map). To do this, students will first have to determine cost per mile (using parameters in the plan) and then calculate totals for each route to compare. At this time gas was 20 cents a gallon, and minimum wage was $0.75/hr. For example, the author shares that spending the night in Tennessee was 100 miles out of the way, which would have cost more than two hour's pay.

Secondary

Hook

Share with the class a personal memory of going on a road trip. Invite them to briefly share their experiences. Ask if along their journey they were treated unjustly. Then tell them that in today's lesson they're going to see how African American people were treated under Jim Crow and how they utilized mathematics to plan a safer route.

Activity No. 1: Independent Reading

The students will read the book individually, either for a brief time in class or as assigned to read at home. Students will summarize the "behind the scenes" mathematical connections they notice for the family to utilize the Green Book.

Activity No. 2: Creating a Plan

In groups or pairs, students research the car (mileage/tank capacity) and speed limit for the 1950s (or use information in the resources) and utilize Google Maps and the Green Book (www.autolife.umd.umich.edu/Race/R_ Casestudy/Negro_motorist_green_bk.htm) to plot out the cities along a route that they determine most plausible to get to Birmingham or from Birmingham to Chicago. Students plot the mileage per day and create a distance-time graph (see resources).

Activity No. 3: Representation

Students, working in pairs or in groups, review their routes for reasonableness (they are not driving too far, they are not stopping too late, and they have enough gas to get to each stop). Students then create their map making their stops accurate to the scale they determine. The students will then transfer to a map (poster or virtual) their color-coded route with labeled stops and their statistical information (graphs/timetable).

The students will present the information to the class and teacher, as the audience mentally checks for reasonableness of the route. The teacher may want to create a rubric for grading including reasoning, computation skills, and data presentation.

Activity No. 4: Comparisons

Students use Google Maps to determine the shortest route without detours (see link in the resources) and make mathematical comparisons between the class's shortest route and this route with appropriate graphs. Students then recap why this longer route was necessary and how they would feel about the unnecessary detours.

Activity No. 5: More Comparisons

Students will compare the cost of the route designed to avoid discrimination and racist encounters with the fastest route (using Google Maps between Chicago and Birmingham). For example, spending the night in Tennessee was 100 miles out of the way (see resources in author interview). At this time gas was 20 cents, and minimum wage was $0.75/hr.

Students should determine the expense and compare that to how many hours of working at minimum wage would be needed to cover the added cost. They could extend their thinking with a debate about the reasonableness of this added expense with arguments rooted in financial literacy and social justice.

Activity No. 6: Challenge

Students will discuss and determine if a "Green Book" is necessary today. If so, what route should be taken and why? Challenge students to create a safe route to their desired vacation spot through group-determined safe cities. Then write or verbally explain why based on recent or current events. Encourage students to use math to determine if this will negatively impact their trip based on time or expense.

Tips for Struggling/Reluctant Learners

Below are some ways that this lesson can be differentiated for struggling or reluctant learners:

- Tier the assignments based on the student's level of readiness: Complete the first leg of the journey (one day's travel), or determine the overall length on the journey with the directions feature in Google Maps for a trip from Chicago directly to Birmingham without detours.
- Utilize flexible grouping: Pair struggling students with stronger students.
- Determine alternatives for presentation modalities: Students may present in Google Slides or Powtoon or on other technological platforms (instead of creating a poster by hand).

Tips for English Language Learners

Below are some ways that this lesson can be differentiated for English language learners:

- Invite students to share their own experiences with discrimination based on their racial or language differences.
- Invite students to connect personally and describe places they feel more comfortable and welcomed.
- Provide translations of the story in students' native language.
- Provide an audio version of the story for students to review before or after class.
- Group students with students who speak their language and English, if possible, for language support.
- Reduce the amount of handwritten work by allowing presentation with technology.

Evaluation of Skills

- Observation: Take notes of students' mathematical reasoning about time and distance.
- Question to check for understanding: "How did you account for . . . ? Why did you decide on . . . ? Would you take this route? Why? Why not?"
- Note-take while listening to student presentation and discussion: Record possible misconceptions to address, concepts to reinforce, and questions for deeper understanding.
- Evaluate written maps and charts for evidence of reasoning and accurate mathematical computations.
- Use the rubric (see Table 8.2) to formally assess the project for reasoning skills and computation.

Additional Online Resources

- Alexander Ramsey Calvin, the author, talks about what the Green Book is and about his story: www.youtube.com/watch?v=Zed2oOfq_-8.
- More information on the *Negro Motorist Green Book*: www.history.com/news/the-green-book-the-black-travelers-guide-to-jim-crow-america.
- Google Maps shortest route: https://goo.gl/maps/cAwv4w3gTSQ2.
- Middle and Secondary Creating a Plan:
    - 1952 Buick gets an average of 16 miles per gallon.
    - 1952 Buick tank lasts about 210 miles.
    - The speed limit at the time was 55 mph on main roads.
    - The most Ruth's father wants to drive during one day is 9 hours.
- Time-distance graph tutorial: www.youtube.com/watch?time_continue=39&v=l93-BkAJ3UY.

Table 8.2. Rubric to Assess Reasoning Skills and Computation

Reasoning	Computation	Effort
High: Logical route based on mathematical reasoning with evidence of stops for basic needs and safety (using the Green Book).	High: Accurate 100% of the time using appropriate mathematical operations for time and distance.	High: Persisting all the way through the lesson, finding logical stops using the Green Book for locations and the directions feature in Google Maps or scale on printed map for distances to make logical decisions.
Mid-level: Somewhat logical route (may have some stops that deviate from direct travel) but based on mathematical reasoning with evidence of stops for basic needs and safety (using the Green Book).	Mid-level: Accurate most of the time (over 70%) using appropriate mathematical operations for time and distance.	Mid-level: Making attempts without request for help, using the Green Book for locations but not always staying on the most logical route with Google Maps, or needing redirecting.
Low: Route is based on guessing or includes stops that are not in the Green Book, or route does not go to desired location.	Low: Often inaccurate or inappropriate mathematical operations for calculating time and distance.	Low: Requesting help or shutting down before using Google Maps and looking through the Green Book for logical stops to create their route.

- United States average prices in 1952: www.reference.com/history/much-did-things-cost-1952-5f6b2d02e9eff03.
- Alternative platforms for presentation: www.codemom.ai/2017/01/15-best-online-presentation-tools-for-students/.

CONCLUDING REMARKS

The historical narrative of injustice to African Americans has been presented with different societal voices depending on who is telling the story. For students who did not grow up in the time of Jim Crow, it is important to understand the perspective of those who endured racism through discrimination. *Ruth and the Green Book* provides a way for students to use mathematics to understand the negative impacts of Jim Crow through something simple like traveling from the character's point of view.

As students engage in the problem of plotting a safe route for the family, they better understand the issue of Jim Crow and hopefully appreciate the strength and determination of the African American people at that time to still travel. Gay (2010) suggests that incorporating stories that give voice to those unrepresented in history is part of being culturally responsive to students.

This connection to understanding discrimination may also lead to discussion and reflection on America's current issues with racism. Again, mathematics can describe some of the negative impacts of racism today, like income, by using a problem-based approach.

REFERENCES

Corp, A. (2017). Tea cakes and sweet potato pie for all: Student responses to African American stories in mathematics. *Curriculum and Teaching Dialogue, 19*(1&2), 35–52.

Delpit, L. (2012). *Multiplication is for white people: Raising expectations for other people's children.* New York: The New Press.

Gay, G. (2010). *Culturally responsive teaching: Theory, research, and practice.* New York: Teachers College Press.

Green, V. (1936–1964). *The negro motorist green book.* New York: Green.

Hefflin, B. R., & Barksdale-Ladd, M. A. (2001). African American children's literature that helps students find themselves: Selection guidelines for grades K–3. *The Reading Teacher, 54*(8), 810–819.

Iliev, N., & D'Angelo, F. (2014). Teaching mathematics through multicultural literature. *Teaching Children Mathematics, 20*(7), 452–457.

Moyer, P. S. (2000). Communicating mathematically: Children's literature as a natural connection. *The Reading Teacher, 54,* 246–256.

9

Harvesting Hope

Equipping Students for Social Activism through a Mathematical Approach to History

Jamie Wong

This chapter examines the history presented in *Harvesting Hope: The Story of Cesar Chavez* with a lens that incorporates mathematics and social activism. Chavez's Delano grape strike march provides a context for students to explore measurements of distance, time, and speed. The project-based learning approach of this chapter emphasizes the use of mathematical literacy techniques and culturally responsive practices.

Problem posing and relevant contexts help engage students from all grade levels. Each activity allows students to take responsibility for their learning and build historical understanding and connections. Students will have opportunities to represent findings with various visual representations and make personal applications to become agents of activism in their communities.

BACKGROUND OF THE LITERATURE

Harvesting Hope: The Story of Cesar Chavez by Kathleen Krull is a biography that recounts the journey of Cesar Chavez, an influential Mexican American historical figure. It provides a holistic view of Chavez's growth through the retelling of his experiences with the harsh realities of poverty and racism, and how activism led to the improvement of the conditions of migrant workers and acknowledgment of their contributions to sharecropping.

This book uses beautiful, colorful illustrations to display the range of emotions and experiences that Chavez encounters throughout his journey. While the text is simple and targets an elementary audience, the lessons from this story are applicable to all ages.

Beginning with Chavez's childhood, the book pays homage to Hispanic culture, highlighting the importance and centrality of family and community. When Chavez experiences hardships in the forms of poverty, homelessness, migration, racism, and bullying, he emphasizes nonviolence and persistence through hard work and dedication. Rather than stigmatize low levels of education, the book honors the necessity of Chavez's decision in his situation. It sheds light on language-shaming, revealing the deficit mindset that teachers often have of English language learners.

Finally, at the young age of twenty, Chavez practices leadership, sacrifice, organization, and activism in a peaceful march to protest injustice. The story ends with victory and hope for many people, yet extends the ideas that empowerment is possible, humility is crucial, and much more is still to be done.

Focusing on Chavez's march, this chapter provides lessons that help students build a tangible understanding of measurement concepts including distance, time, and speed. The lessons use mathematical timelines, maps, and graphs to portray both Chavez's journey and students' creations. Students will have opportunities to create and analyze these visual representations and connect Chavez's march to mathematical problems, personal applications, and ideas for activism.

PEDAGOGICAL APPROACH

This chapter proposes a project-based learning approach that develops literate mathematicians. Project-based learning gives students the role of inquirers, allowing them to take ownership of their direction, process, and product. Rather than solving simple, repetitive mathematics problems, students engage in the content through critical thinking and creative problem solving (Wurdinger, 2016).

Project-based learning provides opportunities for student interest, motivation, and engagement to increase (Verschaffel, Depaepe, & Van Dooren, 2014). With freedom and choice, students will be able to apply mathematics in a context authentic to them. This also provides natural ways to differentiate among students based on ability level, interest, and grouping.

Additionally, developing literate mathematicians is an essential goal in the classroom and can be supported by incorporating the reading of this text, discussing the implications of history, facilitating independent research, creating mathematical representations of statistics, and writing and presenting solutions for each issue. Using research, graphs, and statistics develops a unique form of disciplinary literacy essential to mathematics (Hoffer, 2016).

The nonfiction text provides students with opportunities to make connections between their lives, prior knowledge, social issues, real-world situations, and mathematics content. The literature sets the stage for an organic, meaning-centered environment that sparks students' curiosity (Wilkerson, Fetterly, & Wood, 2015). When students problematize in a realistic context, they can construct mathematical understandings more effectively.

Linguistically and culturally responsive teaching practices are implemented in this chapter by using a story relevant to many students' lives and posing problems that connect with students' interests and identities (Driver & Powell, 2017). By incorporating storytelling and "tapping into questions that tell the students about who they are, the class is turning thoughts, beliefs, and values into concrete mathematical data of great significance" (Torres-Velasquez & Loco, 2004, p. 250).

Students, regardless of their culture, history, or background, will be equipped to not only reason through what justice should look like in various situations, but also how to act on it in a peaceful yet powerful way.

Lesson Objectives

Please note that the NCTM Standards listed are taken from *Principles and Standards for School Mathematics* (National Council of Teachers of Mathematics [NCTM], 2000). These overarching expectations are presented by NCTM as things that "instructional programs from prekindergarten through grade 12 should enable each and every student to" do (p. 32).

These standards may be found in the printed book or on NCTM's website and do not include identification numbers. The sub-standards are not listed due to their specificity to certain grade bands. Depending on grade level and activity, you may find the specific expectations relevant to your students.

Content Overview

Many mathematical projects can be elicited from this story and modified based on students' grade level, needs, and characteristics. Outlined are activities that examine historical and current-day perspectives, allowing the student to take the roles of both researcher and informed activist. Students will have opportunities to collaborate and present, sharing ideas and learning about each other's passions. Each activity may be completed individually or in groups, depending on students' age, needs, and classroom setup. Use chart/poster paper to allow students to present to the whole class. Work can also be displayed around the classroom.

Table 9.1.   Lesson Objectives

Grade Band	Objective	NCTM Standard
Elementary, Middle, Secondary	Students will be able to estimate distances on a map using the given scale and a ruler.	<u>Geometry</u>: Students will specify locations and describe spatial relationships using coordinate geometry and other representational systems.
Elementary, Middle	Students will be able to describe how long a mile is in terms of other units through formal conversions and informal estimates.	<u>Measurement</u>: Students will understand measurable attributes of objects and the units, systems, and processes of measurement.
Elementary, Middle, Secondary	Students will use various tools of measurement (ruler, tape measure, timer) to measure distance and calculate speed.	<u>Measurement</u>: Students will apply appropriate techniques, tools, and formulas to determine measurements.
Elementary, Middle, Secondary	Students will analyze the information they collect and synthesize it into appropriate mathematical representations.	<u>Data Analysis</u>: Students will select and use appropriate statistical methods to analyze data.
Middle, Secondary	Students will pose and solve mathematical problems based off of Cesar Chavez's story and personal interest.	<u>Data Analysis</u>: Students will formulate questions that can be addressed with data and collect, organize, and display relevant data to answer them.
Middle, Secondary	Students will propose solutions for problems posed and extend them to make connections to the real world.	<u>Data Analysis</u>: Students will develop and evaluate inferences and predictions that are based on data.

In *Harvesting Hope*, Cesar Chavez's peaceful protest was a march. Because of this, the mathematical connections pull heavily from the measurement content area. Students will learn how to measure distance, speed, and maps. These measurement skills will be extended to real-world, everyday applications. Additionally, heavy emphasis is placed on graphic representations to provide supplemental visual support for students' claims and solutions. By communicating their findings in various ways, students will be able to make clear connections.

Some of these activities may include a proposal for a solution or change. Before implementing, contact your administrators, local policymakers, parents, and community members to see if students can have any opportunities to share their findings with a larger audience. Part of empowering students is bringing the hypothetical to action. These activities will have much more meaning if students see the potential impact their work can have on real-world situations and problems.

Materials/Supplies

- Krull, K. (2003). *Harvesting hope: The story of Cesar Chavez*. Orlando, FL: Harcourt.
- Devices with Internet access
- Library books and encyclopedias
- Letter and Timeline from Chavez's peaceful protest (Resource No. 1)
- Map of Chavez's march route (Resource No. 2)
- How Long Is a Mile? Chart (Resource No. 3)
- Measuring Speed Chart (Resource No. 4)
- Mathematics Problem-Posing Recording Sheet (Resource No. 5)
- Rulers and measuring tapes
- Stopwatches
- Notebooks and paper
- Graph/chart paper
- Writing utensils, scissors, glue
- Poster board

SEQUENCE OF ACTIVITIES

Elementary

Hook: Historical Understanding and Connections

Ask students what the farthest distance they have ever walked is. What was the situation? Was it worth it to walk that far or long? Allow students to swap stories. Depending on age, their understandings of distance may differ. Then ask them: "What could motivate you to walk a long time? How far or long would you be willing to walk for it?" Tie this into questions that scaffold understanding of 300 miles or 25 days:

- What would you walk one mile for? What about ten miles? What about 100 miles? 300 miles?
- What would you walk ten minutes for? One hour? One day? 25 days?

It may be helpful to think of a well-known city in your area approximately 300 miles away and ask them what it would take for them to walk this distance. Then set the scene for Cesar Chavez's march.

Activity No. 1: Story Read-Aloud

The teacher will read the story to the class or ask for student volunteers. Begin with a simple read-aloud with students for the first round. To engage students further and deepen understanding, reread the story and have different students act out each character. Every student should take an active role at some point in the story.

Activity No. 2: Timeline and Map

The teacher will introduce the timeline Cesar Chavez sent to his supporters with information on the dates and stops in the march (page 3 of Resource No. 1). In small groups, students will receive a map of this route (Resource No. 2). Using the map scale and a measuring tool, students will label the distances between each city.

Activity No. 3: Measuring Distance

Ask students: How long is a mile? If there are any places one mile from your school, consider pulling those in to build real connections to what students know. The teacher will then introduce the formal measurement conversions of a mile: 1,760 yards, 5,280 feet, or 63,360 inches. Individually, with partners, or in a small group, students will then compare the distance of a mile to informal measurements of objects in the classroom. A whole-class demonstration may be used for younger grade levels.

Students will measure things in the classroom and record them on a chart (Resource No. 3). Using division and multiplication, students will show how many of this object are in one mile. Then students will extend this to show how many of this object would cover Chavez's march (300 miles!). An example is included in the evaluation portion of this chapter, Figure 9.1. Students should present their findings with the class so that more connections to the distance of one mile are made.

Activity No. 4: Measuring Speed

Mark off a certain distance in the classroom with tape. Depending on challenge level, use yards, feet, or inches with differing levels of divisibility.

Divide the class into pairs and have half the class walk the distance at a time, with their partner timing them. Students will record and use this information to estimate how long it would take to walk a mile (Resource No. 4). An example is shown in the evaluation section in Figure 9.2.

Students will extend this estimate to how long it would take to walk 300 miles. Convert from seconds to minutes, hours, days, and weeks as necessary. Again, this can be done with the whole class with one or two students demonstrating, depending on the level of guidance students need. Students can compare with partners or small groups to see how their walking speeds differ.

Activity No. 5: Graphic Representations

Students will create a graph to represent the information they have collected so far (the type of graph will depend on grade level). This may cover distance or length of time walking. Once students create a graph, they will swap with a partner who created a different type of graph and come up with one question. Examples of graphs and questions can be seen in Figure 9.3. Graphs can also be presented to the whole class or displayed in the classroom.

Middle

Hook: Historical Understandings and Connections

Find a city that is approximately 300 miles away that students are familiar with. Pose the question: "What could motivate you to walk 300 miles?" Allow students to make estimates on how long it would take.

Activity No. 1: Story Read-Aloud

The teacher will read the story to the class or ask for student volunteers.

Activity No. 2: Letters, Timeline, and Map

The teacher will introduce the letters and timeline Cesar Chavez sent to his supporters with information on the dates and stops in the march (page 3 of Resource No. 1). In small groups, students will read the letters and receive a map of this route (Resource No. 2). Using the map scale and a measuring tool, students will label the distances between each city.

Activity No. 3: Measuring Distance

Ask students: How long is a mile? If there are any places one mile from your school, consider pulling those in to build real connections to what students know. The teacher will then introduce the formal measurement conversions of a mile: 1,760 yards, 5,280 feet, or 63,360 inches. Individually, with partners, or in a small group, students will then compare the distance of a mile to informal measurements of objects in the classroom.

Students will measure things in the classroom and record them on a chart (Resource No. 3). Using proportions, students will show how many of this object are in one mile. Then, students will extend this to show how many of this object would cover Chavez's march (300 miles!). Students should present their findings with the class so that more connections to the distance of one mile are made.

Activity No. 4: Measuring Speed

Mark off a certain distance in the classroom (or outside if permissible) with tape. Depending on challenge level, use yards, feet, or inches with differing levels of divisibility. Divide the class into pairs and have half the class walk the distance at a time, with their partner timing them.

Students will record and use this information to estimate how long it would take to walk a mile (Resource No. 4). Students will extend this estimate to how long it would take to walk 300 miles. Convert using proportions from seconds to minutes, hours, days, and weeks as necessary. Students can also write equations to represent the situation.

Activity No. 5: Trip Snapshot and Gallery Walk

Students will create a poster or presentation to represent the information they have collected so far. The final product should be a trip snapshot that shows all the basic information of the march, including distance, length of time walking, average speeds, and more. Students must use a variety of representations in their product (graphs, tables, equations).

Once all students are finished, all final products will be displayed. Students will do a gallery walk, examining their peers' work. Each student should come up with one observation or question about a peer's product, which may compare or contrast the mathematics and representations used.

Extension: Problem Posing

If you want to extend this lesson to make it more personal for students, any of the following activities may be used:

- *Activity 1: (Re)Read Aloud and Mathematics Problem Posing* The teacher will (re)read the story to the class or ask for student volunteers. As the story is read, each student will be given a Mathematics Problem-Posing Recording Sheet (Resource No. 5). Students will jot down mathematical questions or problems based on the scenarios in the story. This may need to be modeled by the teacher providing examples before or as the book is read. Then, in small groups, students will share their questions and record what additional information is necessary to solve the mathematical problem. If students have similar questions, they may work with partners or small groups.
- *Activity 2: Research* Students will be given access to the library or devices with Internet access. If this is new for students, consider doing a short lesson with your school's librarian on digital literacy and how to cite sources correctly. They will research the information needed to solve their mathematical problems and record it on the sheet from Activity 1. Once they think they have obtained enough information, they will check with the teacher. Note that some students' questions may need to be refined depending on the information available. Teachers are recommended to check in with each individual student before or as research begins. An example is in Figure 9.4 in the evaluation portion of this chapter.
- *Activity 3: Problem Solving and Presentation* Students will use their newfound information to solve the problem they posed. At least two mathematical representations (graphs, tables, equations, mappings) must be used. Their product may be on chart paper, a poster, or even a digital presentation slide. They will share their findings with the class. A sample rubric to evaluate presentations is in Figure 9.5 in the evaluation portion of this chapter.
- *Activity 4: Problem Extension* Students may do self- or peer-evaluation. Based on their problem and solution, what further questions does this spark? Can the information obtained be used to solve a further problem? What limitations does the solution have? By examining their work critically, students can see how real-world problems do not always have a "neat" solution.

Secondary

Hook: Historical Understanding and Connections

Find a city that is approximately 300 miles away that students are familiar with. Pose the question: "What could motivate you to walk 300 miles?" Allow students to make estimates of how long it would take.

Activity No. 1: Story Read-Aloud

Students will read the story independently or in small groups.

Activity No. 2: Letters, Timeline, and Map

The teacher will introduce the letters and timeline Cesar Chavez sent to his supporters with information on the dates and stops in the march (page 3 of Resource No. 1). In small groups, students will read the letters and receive a map of this route (Resource No. 2). Using the map scale and a measuring tool, students will label the distances between each city.

Activity No. 3: Measuring Speed

Find a place outdoors or in the hallways if possible. Give students a measuring tool and a timer. Students will calculate their speed with a partner, using any distance and time they choose. Using proportions and equations, students will use this information to estimate how long it would take to walk a mile (Resource No. 4). Students will extend this estimate to how long it would take to walk 300 miles. Convert using proportions from seconds to minutes, hours, days, and weeks as necessary. Students can also write equations to represent the situation.

Activity No. 4: Google Maps Comparison

Students will return to their maps and label the estimated time it would take to walk between each city. Once the map is complete, students will be given access to a device that has Google Maps. The students will compare their findings with the reality: How accurate are their measures of distance and walking speed? Students will write their findings on the back of their map, highlighting mathematical differences and brainstorming what might account for the differences.

This is a form of self-assessment, as students will see how accurate their work was. It also helps students understand that real-life implications may not always look like the mathematical model.

Extension: Personal Activism

If you want to extend this lesson to make it more personal for students, any of the following activities may be used:

- *Activity 1: (Re)Read Aloud and Identify Issue* The students will (re)read the story. As the story is read, students will record Cesar Chavez's motivations and experiences with the Delano grape march, answering the questions: Why did Chavez lead a march for farm workers? What personal experiences contributed to his desire for justice? Then students will brainstorm an issue they personally are passionate about and answer the same two questions. This may be done individually, in pairs, or in small groups.
- *Activity 2: March Research and Planning* Students will create a plan for their own march regarding their chosen issue. Students will be given access to the library or devices with Internet access. If this is new for students, consider doing a short lesson with your school's librarian on digital literacy and how to cite sources correctly. Some guidelines for students include: What statistics support your stance on your issue? What is your proposed change or solution? What information would you want to communicate with supporters? (Have them review the letters that Chavez wrote to his audience. This may also be in partnership with the students' English teachers on persuasive letter writing.) Include supporting information about the beginning and ending locations, stops, distances, timeline, and significance of your route.
- *Activity 3: Presentation* Students will compile their newfound information to create a presentation to share with the class. Their product may be a poster, digital presentation slide, video, letter, or more (have students discuss their desired product with the teacher). Students will give a ten- to fifteen-minute presentation explaining the background of the issue, their personal motivation, and proposed change. Various mathematical representations should be used, including statistics, graphs, tables, and more. All proposals must be strongly supported by mathematical proof. A sample rubric to evaluate presentations is in figure 9.6 in the evaluation portion of this chapter. If it is possible, make this activity even more meaningful by inviting community members or key policymakers.

Otherwise, have students learn how to contact these people, and allow them to do so (again, it may be helpful to have English teachers work on this interdisciplinary piece).

Tips for Struggling/Reluctant Readers

To differentiate this lesson for struggling or reluctant readers, allow various groupings based on students' needs. Support students by reading the book more than once in different settings and refer to the text often. Allow students to check out the books and take them home, and make sure the pictures are visible to all. Once the book is read, showing supplementary videos about Cesar Chavez or having students act the story out may also provide positive reinforcement.

Tips for English Language Learners

Create a word wall for the key terms from this book and put them in a visible place in the classroom. Include words, definitions, translations, and pictures on each card. Allow students to collaborate and be grouped based on their needs. If students are doing research, allow them to use websites or books in their native language if they translate the key points for their final project. Emphasize the use of visuals and graphics to provide another accessible form of communication.

Evaluation of Skills

Many of the activities outlined in this chapter do not have one correct answer. The structure of project-based learning allows students to choose how to respond. Providing students with guidelines, checklists, and rubrics will allow them to self-assess, peer-assess, and understand clear expectations. A portfolio-based approach also allows students to show a holistic view of their work, rather than just a summative evaluation at the end. Teachers are encouraged to have meetings with students as they work and evaluate formatively throughout each activity.

Students should be given ample time to practice before jumping into the final projects.

For students to know how to measure, the teacher should model and guide students and then give them plenty of time in class to try. Additionally, research should be carefully monitored. Teachers must help students access quality resources and ensure that time online is not being abused. Examples of student work and assessments follow:

Elementary:

One mile is equal to 1,760 yards, 5,280 feet, and 63,360 inches.

Feet

A desk measures about two feet.

There are 5,280 feet in one mile. So, it would take about 2,640   desks to

(how many) (object)

measure one mile.

Show Work:

5,280 feet / 2 feet = 2,640 desks

2,640 desks * 300 = 792,000 desks

Cesar Chavez walked for about 300 miles. That would mean he walked the distance of 792,000 desks lined up!

(how many) (object)

Figure 9.1. Example of Measuring Distance Activity. *Author created.*

Example:

Mary walked 10 feet in 7 seconds.

How long would it take for you to walk a mile? 61.6 minutes, or a little over 1 hour.

Show work:

5,280 feet in a mile

5,280/10 = 528

528 * 7 seconds = 3,696 seconds

3,696 seconds / 60 seconds = 61.6 minutes

How long would it take for you to walk 300 miles? Almost 13 days of nonstop walking!

Show work:

61.6 minutes * 300 = 18,480 minutes

18,480 / 60 minutes = 308 hours

308 hours / 24 = 12.8333 days

Figure 9.2.   Example of Measuring Speed Activity. *Author created.*

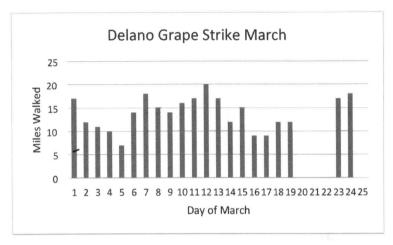

Question: How many days did the marchers walk over 10 miles?

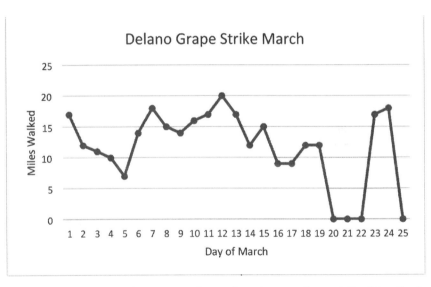

Question: Why were there some days when the marchers walked 0 miles?

Figure 9.3. Graphic Representations Examples. *Author created.*

Middle School:

What questions do you have?	What guesses do you have?
1. How much have farm workers' wages improved since Cesar Chavez's time? 2. How many tons of grapes rotted?	1. 10 times! 2. Thousands

What information do you need?	What is your research plan?
1. How much farm workers got paid back then, and how much farm workers are paid now. 2. How quickly grapes rot; the total amount of time Chavez and his team marched.	1. Use an internet search to look up a history of farm worker wages; read more details on the deal Chavez signed 2. Research agricultural websites

Information found:

1. From https://fred.stlouisfed.org/series/FEDMINFRMWG, in 1967, the minimum wage for farm workers was $1.00. In 2018, that has increased to $7.25.
2. According to https://newrepublic.com/article/132142/grape-pickers-strike, in Chavez's time, the average grape-picker was getting $1.20 per hour.
3.

Figure 9.4. Mathematics Problem-Posing Recording Sheet Sample. *Author created.*

CATEGORY	4	3	2	1
Problem Posing	Problem posed is mathematical in nature, open-ended, and drawn from the text.	Problem posed is mathematical in nature, drawn from the text, but not open-ended.	Problem posed is mathematical in nature, but not drawn from the text nor open-ended.	Problem posed is not mathematical.
Research	Various (3+) reputable sources were used in research and cited. Information contributed to solving of problem.	Some (2+) reputable sources were used in research and cited. Information contributed to solving of problem.	One reputable source was used in research and cited. Information contributed to solving of problem.	No outside sources were used, or information was irrelevant to the problem\'s solution.
Presentation	Presentation includes 2+ representations. The product is clear - easy to read and understand.	Presentation includes 1+ representations. The product is clear - easy to read and understand.	Presentation only includes the solution without other representations. The product is difficult to read or understand.	The presentation does not include a solution, or cannot be read or understood.

Figure 9.5. Mathematics Problem-Posing Presentation Sample Rubric. *Author created.*

Secondary:

CATEGORY	4	3	2	1
Product Type	Product has been approved by instructor, and is conducive to clear communication of mathematics. Product is easy to read and understand.	Product has been approved by instructor, and is conducive to clear communication of mathematics. Product is mostly easy to read and understand.	Product has been approved by instructor, and is conducive to clear communication of mathematics. Product is difficult to read and understand.	Product has been approved by instructor, but does not allow for clear communication of mathematics. Product is difficult to read and understand.
Critical Elements	Product includes ALL of the following: mathematical statistics of the background of the issue, personal motivation, proposed solution, and supporting mathematical representations.	Product includes 4 of the following: mathematical statistics of the background of the issue, personal motivation, proposed solution, and supporting mathematical representations.	Product includes 2 of 4 of the following: mathematical statistics of the background of the issue, personal motivation, proposed solution, and supporting mathematical representations.	Product includes 1 of 4 of the following: mathematical statistics of the background of the issue, personal motivation, proposed solution, and supporting mathematical representations.
Mathematical Support and Accuracy	Mathematics is used throughout the presentation to provide strong support. The mathematics and vocabulary used is accurate.	Mathematics is used throughout the presentation to provide support. The mathematics and vocabulary used is accurate.	Mathematics is used throughout the presentation to provide support. The mathematics and vocabulary used have some mistakes.	Mathematics is rarely used throughout the presentation. The mathematics and vocabulary used have multiple mistakes.
Research	Various (5+) reputable sources were used in research and correctly cited. Information drawn from these sources contributed to rationale and mathematical proof.	Various (4+) reputable sources were used in research and correctly cited. Information drawn from these sources contributed to rationale and mathematical proof.	Some (3+) reputable sources were used in research and correctly cited. Information drawn from these sources mostly contributed to rationale and mathematical proof.	Few (1+) reputable sources were used in research and correctly cited. Information drawn from these sources somewhat contributed to rationale and mathematical proof.
Presentation	The presentation is within the time limit of 15 minutes. Eye contact and voice volume are appropriate. Overall persuasive and enthusiastic.	The presentation does not meet the time limit of 15 minutes. Eye contact and voice volume are appropriate. Overall persuasive and enthusiastic.	The presentation does not meet the time limit of 15 minutes. Eye contact and voice volume are lacking. Overall persuasive and enthusiastic.	The presentation does not meet the time limit of 15 minutes. Eye contact and voice volume are lacking. Not persuasive and enthusiastic.

Figure 9.6. Mathematics Personal Activism Presentation Sample Rubric. *Author created.*

Additional Resources

- **Resource No. 1:** Letter and Timeline from Cesar Chavez's march can be found here: libraries.ucsd.edu/farmworkermovement/essays/essays/MillerArchive/016%20Letter%20From%20Cesar%20Chavez%20To%20Friends.pdf.
- **Resource No. 2:** Map of Cesar Chavez's Delano Grape Strike March Pudlin, A. (2015, March 31). Cesar Chavez and the Grape Strike March: From Delano to Sacramento. [Blog post]. Retrieved from igotcharts.tumblr.com/post/115154341182/happy-cesar-chavez-day-heres-a-map-highlighting

- Resource No. 3: How Long Is a Mile?

TEXTBOX 9.1.   RESOURCE NO. 3: HOW LONG IS A MILE?

One mile is equal to _____ yards, _____ feet, and _____ inches.

Yards

_____ measures about _____ yards.
     (object)   (length)
 	
There are _____ yards in one mile. So it would take about
    (how many)
_____ to measure one mile.
    (object)
 	
Show Work:
 	
Cesar Chavez walked for about 300 miles. That would mean he walked the distance of _____ _____ lined up!
                      (how many)   (object)

Feet

_____ measures about _____ feet.
     (object)   (length)
 	
There are _____ feet in one mile. So it would take about
    (how many)
_____ to measure one mile.
    (object)
 	
Show Work:
 	
Cesar Chavez walked for about 300 miles. That would mean he walked the distance of _____ _____ lined up!
                      (how many)   (object)

Inches

_____ measures about _____ inches.
    (object)   length)

There are _____ feet in one mile. So it would take about
    (how many)
_____ _____ to measure one mile.
    (object)

Show Work:

Cesar Chavez walked for about 300 miles. That would mean he walked the distance of _____ _____ lined up!
                    (how many)   (object)

- Resource No. 4: Measuring Speed

TEXTBOX 9.2. RESOURCE NO. 4: MEASURING SPEED

_____ walked _____ in _____ seconds.
(Partner's name)   (distance)

How long would it take for you to walk a mile?
Show work:

How long would it take for you to walk in Cesar Chavez's march (300 miles)?

Show work:

• Resource No. 5: Mathematics Problem-Posing Recording Sheet

Table 9.2.   Resource No. 5: Mathematics Problem-Posing Recording Sheet

What questions do you have?	What guesses do you have?
What information do you need?	What is your research plan?
Information found:	

CONCLUDING REMARKS

By incorporating multicultural literature, problem solving, and project-based learning, this chapter proposes rich mathematical tasks that engage students in relevant and authentic contexts. The activities scaffold students' tangible understanding of this historical event and application to current-day events. While the primary mathematical focus of this chapter is measurement, students' problem posing and activism plans may provide connections and extensions to many other concepts.

The goals of these activities are to support students in developing identities as literate mathematicians and elicit diverse voices in rich mathematical discourse. By taking inspiration from Cesar Chavez's life, students can be empowered to think through practical ways they can be agents of change in their communities.

REFERENCES

Driver, M. K., & Powell, S. R. (2017). Culturally and linguistically responsive schema intervention: Improving word problem solving for English language learners with mathematics difficulty. *Learning Disability Quarterly, 40*(1), 41–53. doi. org/10.1177/0731948716646730.

Hoffer, W. W. (2016). *Developing literate mathematicians: A guide for integrating language and literacy instruction into secondary mathematics.* Reston, VA: NCTM.

Krull, K. (2003). *Harvesting hope: The story of Cesar Chavez.* Orlando, FL: Harcourt.

National Council of Teachers of Mathematics. (2000). *Principles and standards for school mathematics.* Reston, VA: NCTM.

Torres-Velasquez, D., & Lobo, G. (2004). Culturally responsive mathematics teaching and English language learners. *Teaching Children Mathematics, 11*(5), 249–255. Retrieved from http://www.k12.wa.us/BEST/Symposium/2b.pdf

Verschaffel, L., Depaepe, F., & Van Dooren, W. (2014). Mathematical problem solving. In P. Andrews & T. Rowland (Eds.), *Master class in mathematics education: International perspectives on teaching and learning* (pp. 113–124). London: Bloomsbury. Retrieved from nces.ed.gov/fastfacts/display.asp?id=372

Wilkerson, T. L., Fetterly, J., & Wood, B. (2015). Problem posing and problem solving. In J. A. Hayn, J. S. Kaplan, A. L. Nolen, and H. A. Olyey (Eds.), *Young adult nonfiction* (pp. 67–82). Lanham, MD: Rowman & Littlefield.

Wurdinger, S. D. (2016). *The power of project-based learning: Helping students develop important life skills.* Lanham, MD: Rowman & Littlefield.

Maya's Blanket

Applying Mathematics to Solve Everyday Problems

Amy K. Corp

This chapter describes how to utilize the story *Maya's Blanket* to demonstrate the power of mathematics to solve everyday problems. The problem in the story is what to do with a beloved blanket that is deteriorating over time. Maya and her abuelita (grandmother) creatively repurpose the blanket into a new item each time it deteriorates.

The lessons in this chapter are crafted for students to understand and replicate the mathematics used to make the transformations seen in the book, for example from blanket to dress, and to recognize that mathematics helps us solve everyday problems. Younger students use mathematics to describe and compare size. Older elementary students use operations and measuring of surface area to replicate one of the blanket's transformations. Middle school and high school students use mathematical reasoning to design and describe their own transformation of a beloved item into something useful for today.

BACKGROUND OF THE LITERATURE

Maya's grandmother made her a special blanket. Over the course of the book and Maya's childhood, the blanket is transformed into a dress, skirt, shawl, scarf, hair ribbon, and bookmark. The story is written as a memoir of her special blanket and her memories of Abuelita.

The illustrations in the story are authentic and affirming to the Hispanic culture. They convey warm family bonds and how creative the characters are in repurposing the material of the beloved blanket. The English version includes the Spanish word for each new object and defines the word within the sentence with context clues or the English word.

The text of the story also uses repetition to increase fluency and strengthens sequencing. *Maya's Blanket* is also available in Spanish and would be a welcome addition in the classroom library for Spanish readers. Some themes in this story are strong grandmother-granddaughter bonds, creative/artistic work, problem solving by recycling/repurposing, and a passion for reading, writing, and drawing.

Utilizing a story builds prior knowledge for the contexts of the problems that are solved through the use of mathematics (Moyer, 2000) unseen in the story but that will be practiced in this lesson. Also, a story helps students find commonalities between students' lives and the characters and/or culture featured in the book (Corp, 2017; Hefflin & Barksdale-Ladd, 2001).

In this story, some connections to students' lives may be love between grandmother and grandchild; reusing material; being creative; appreciating family; and loving to read, draw, or write. Students who are not native English speakers hear the English language (including terms used specifically in mathematics) in context, with repetition on several pages, and in discussion of the story, thus creating a stronger authentic understanding of English and mathematical words.

Reinforcing language through literature is a powerful way to increase students' speaking and comprehension of language while learning the content (Pérez, 2012). In working with kindergarteners, Hassinger-Das, Jordan, and Dyson (2015) found that using storybooks boosted mathematical vocabulary more than instruction without stories.

PEDAGOGICAL APPROACH

This chapter proposes a collaborative problem-based model implementing the constructivist learning approach to mathematical concepts. First students listen to the story, which will be the basis for the problem they will collaboratively solve. By listening to the story together and solving problems similar to the character, students have opportunities to engage in conversations about the text and the problem using vocabulary and mathematical language (Pérez, 2012).

Utilizing the problem-solving model, students must critically think about the story and how mathematics helped Maya and her grandmother change the blanket into a new and usable item each time it needed to be recycled. Critically thinking about problem solving in a story is powerful (Boaler, 2015) because children are naturally acting as the character and determining what she (Maya) knew mathematically that was not expressed in the text of the story in order to solve the problem of saving the deteriorating blanket.

Starting with a story also helps students to create mathematical connections. In the constructivist learning approach, students use this critical thinking to engage their imagination and visualize what mathematics the character used. Visualizing in mathematics engages the brain in deeper thinking and helps students to better understand a variety of mathematical concepts (Van Garderen, 2006; Van de Walle, Karp, Bay-Williams, Wray, & Brown, 2007). In this chapter, students are encouraged to visualize, to act out, and to draw out how Maya used mathematics to create a new smaller form from the original. Students may connect to counting, ratios, subtraction, symmetry, surface area, scale, nets, percents, and fractions.

Students will collaborate with a partner to reenact one transformation (for example, from skirt to shawl) with tools of their choice (cloth, construction paper, grid paper, dry erase board) before moving on to design their own plan for repurposing something special to them. Students will discuss their ideas, and after producing their reenactment, they will explain how they were able to solve the issue of size reduction with mathematics. Students are also encouraged to compare their plans and explanations with others. When students problem solve and explain, they are gaining a better mathematical understanding through metacognition and conjecture (Boaler, 2015).

Having students connect to real-life problems engages students in the application of mathematical skills and knowledge. Students connect to their own lives by designing a plan and thinking mathematically about how to repurpose a towel, blanket, or item of clothing into a useful and meaningful item for their current use or wear. Connecting to their personal life is culturally responsive and helps students see mathematics as part of their life (Corp, 2018; Iliev & D'Angelo, 2014).

By using a story that is culturally affirming and connecting it to real-life problems, the action of solving these problems creates connections to many students' lives and experiences and is one way to be culturally responsive to students (Gay, 2010). Since the mathematics happens within the warm family relationship between Maya and her grandmother, students from all cultures should connect, as most children are fond of their grandmothers.

Throughout the lesson, language is reinforced through listening to the story, speaking with a partner and peers (while solving the problem), during explanations, and connections to their own personal stories. These are all strategies for supporting English language learners (Robertson, 2009). Since the mathematics is situated within the context of story, students hear and use language, not just numbers, to think about and solve mathematical problems.

The text in the story affirms the Hispanic culture because the Spanish version of the word for the object is used first and repeated in each transformation so students hear the words again and again in context. The book is also available in Spanish and encourages students (Spanish speaking and non-Spanish speaking) to appreciate the Spanish language and to find several cognates (words that are the same in both languages).

Creating a simple paper model of the objects with the English and Spanish word written on them and displaying them at eye level would also help English language learners and continue to affirm the Spanish language.

Lesson Objectives

NCTM Process Standards:

- Problem solving:
  - The student will build new mathematical knowledge through problem solving.
  - The student will solve problems that arise in mathematics and in other contexts.
  - The student will apply and adapt a variety of appropriate strategies to solve problems.
- Communication:
  - The student will organize and consolidate their mathematical thinking through communication.
  - The student will communicate their mathematical thinking coherently and clearly to peers, teachers, and others.
  - The student will analyze and evaluate the mathematical thinking and strategies of others.
  - The student will use the language of mathematics to express mathematical ideas precisely.
- Connections:
  - The student will recognize and use connections among mathematical ideas.
  - The student will understand how mathematical ideas interconnect and build on one another to produce a coherent whole.
  - The student will recognize and apply mathematics in contexts outside of mathematics.
- Representations:
  - The student will select, apply, and translate among mathematical representations to solve problems.
  - The student will use representations to model and interpret physical, social, and mathematical phenomena.

NCTM Content Standards

- Pre-K–2:
  - The student will connect number words and numerals to the quantities they represent, using various physical models and representations.
  - The student will understand the effects of adding and subtracting whole numbers.
  - The student will use a variety of methods and tools to compute, including objects, mental computation, and estimation.
  - The student will recognize, name, compare, and sort two-dimensional shapes.
  - The student will create mental images of geometric shapes using spatial memory and spatial visualization.
  - The student will recognize and represent shapes from different perspectives.
  - The student will relate ideas in geometry to ideas in number and measurement.
  - The student will recognize the attributes of length and area.
  - The student will compare and order objects according to these attributes.
  - The student will understand how to measure using nonstandard and standard units.
  - The student will select an appropriate unit and tool for the attribute being measured.
- 3–5:
  - The student will recognize equivalent representations for the same number and generate them by decomposing and composing numbers.
  - The student will understand the effects of multiplying and dividing whole numbers.
  - The student will identify and use relationships between operations, such as division as the inverse of multiplication, to solve problems.
  - The student will develop and use strategies to estimate the results of whole-number computations and to judge the reasonableness of such results.
  - The student will investigate, describe, and reason about the results of subdividing, combining, and transforming shapes.
  - The student will use geometric models to solve problems in other areas of mathematics, such as number and measurement.
  - The student will recognize geometric ideas and relationships and apply them to other disciplines and to problems that arise in the classroom or in everyday life.

○ The student will understand such attributes as length and area and select the appropriate type of unit for measuring each attribute.

○ The student will explore what happens to measurements of a two-dimensional shape such as its perimeter and area when the shape is changed in some way.

• 6–8:

○ The student will develop meaning for percents greater than 100 and less than 1.

○ The student will understand and use ratios and proportions to represent quantitative relationships.

○ The student will use the associative and commutative properties of addition and multiplication and the distributive property of multiplication over addition to simplify computations with integers.

○ The student will understand and use the inverse relationships of addition and subtraction, multiplication and division to simplify computations and solve problems.

○ The student will understand relationships among the angles, side lengths, perimeters, areas, and volumes of similar objects.

○ The student will use two-dimensional representations of three-dimensional objects to visualize and solve problems such as those involving surface area and volume.

○ The student will recognize and apply geometric ideas and relationships in areas outside the mathematics classroom, such as art, science, and everyday life.

○ The student will understand, select, and use units of appropriate size and type to measure perimeter, area, surface area, and volume.

• 9–12:

○ The student will analyze properties and determine attributes of two- and three-dimensional objects.

○ The student will understand and represent translations, reflections, rotations, and dilations of objects in the plane by using sketches, coordinates, vectors, function notation, and matrices.

○ The student will use various representations to help understand the effects of simple transformations and their compositions.

○ The student will use geometric models to gain insights into, and answer questions in, other areas of mathematics.

○ The student will use geometric ideas to solve problems in, and gain insights into, other disciplines and other areas of interest such as art and architecture.

○ The students will make decisions about units and scales that are appropriate for problem situations involving measurement.

Content Overview

In this lesson, students across all grade levels will solve the problem of how to repurpose the blanket in the story into another item using mathematical processes. Students will do more in-depth thinking, visualization, and computation based on what is appropriate for the students and grade level.

The lesson focuses on using mathematical processes with their content knowledge. For example, kindergarteners will reason and communicate utilizing counting, while fourth graders may use reasoning and representation by calculating surface area through repeated addition or multiplication.

Middle school students will reason and communicate to practice surface area strategies with a partner, and high schoolers will make connections to scale to create three-dimensional representations and communicate their own ideas.

Materials/Supplies

- Brown, M. (2015) *Maya's blanket*. New York: Lee & Low Books.
- Words in Spanish and in English on the board with picture
- Dry erase boards/markers
- Unifix cubes
- Graph paper
- Construction paper
- (Optional) remnants of cloth
- Writing utensils
- Notebook paper or math journal

Spanish words: manta (blanket), vestido (dress), falda (skirt), rebozo (shawl), bufanda (scarf), cinta (ribbon), marcador de libros (bookmark)

SEQUENCE OF ACTIVITIES

K–2

Hook

Have students bring a favorite childhood item (blanket, pillow, stuffed animal, etc.) or photo of the item with them to class and tell why it is special. Invite students to turn and talk to a partner for one minute about their favorite item. If time allows, ask a few students to share aloud. Utilize students' interest in their favorite item to introduce and connect to the story *Maya's Blanket*.

Activity No. 1: Read-Aloud

Read aloud the story connecting to literacy practices like predictions from the cover, a picture walk through the book to provide prior knowledge and vocabulary, defining and practicing the Spanish words, and asking cause and effect questions at appropriate times (for example, "Why do you think the blanket was changed to a dress?"). After the story, ask questions that connect to mathematics. "What happened to the size of the material from the original blanket? Why? How do you know? How do you think Maya and Abuelita changed the size?"

Activity No. 2: Partner Collaboration

Partner the students so all students are supported (English language learners with native speaker and mixed-ability pairing). Ask students to think about the blanket and one transformation: when the blanket changed to something new.

To support younger students, use large paper manipulatives of the sizes below. A Unifix cube (the unit) is about 1 inch. Every group should have a model of the blanket (a large paper, perhaps even with units marked, to represent 8 feet x 10 feet). Give each group two models to help them visualize their thinking. For example, hand them the model for the shawl and hair scarf to compare.

- Blanket (8 × 10 unit rectangle)
- Dress (7 × 9 irregular polygon)
- Skirt (4 × 6 unit rectangle)
- Shawl (3 × 6 unit rectangle)
- Scarf (2 × 5 unit rectangle)
- Hair ribbon (1 × 4 unit rectangle)
- Bookmark (1/2 × 3 unit rectangle)

Write these questions on the board for students to explore with their partner: What happened to the blanket? About how much material was discarded (thrown away because it could not be used)? How could you find out? Encourage students to answer the questions written on the board with paper models of the items and verbal explanations based on what they see and think.

Activity No. 3: Reasoning and Action

Regroup students together for a short discussion of the answers, and record their ideas. Possible methods for solving include measuring length, perimeter, or area and subtracting to find out, or students could compare the difference in size by putting the smaller model over the larger one and counting the amount of units needed to cover the area that is still visible.

For young students, start with measuring the length and noticing how the length gets smaller as the object gets smaller. More advanced students might measure the perimeter or the surface area to explain how it is getting smaller. If time allows, encourage students to do more than one transformation.

Activity No. 4: Presentation

Have students return to their partners and use their plan to show what happened and how much material was discarded (even if you adjust it to what length of material was discarded). Students should explain what they did to solve the problem to their partner and take turns so each student answers the questions and explains how they arrived at that answer.

Advanced students could represent their findings by drawing in their math journal with labels and/or short sentences. The teacher observes, listens, questions, and takes note of how students are thinking and implementing their plan.

3–5

Hook

As the teacher, share a personal memory of a beloved blanket, pillow, or T-shirt. Allow time for students to turn and talk to a partner about a similar memory. Ask if any of them have remade their special item into something else. Then introduce the story of how Maya repurposes her special blanket. Read the story, asking what the Spanish words mean from the context, gathering predictions, and ending with comprehension questions.

Activity No. 1: Discussion and Plan

Ask students to make connections between the story and mathematics. How did Maya use math to make part of her blanket into something new? How could you figure out how to change the blanket (manta) into the shawl (rebozo)? Give wait time, and record possible plans. Plans may include measuring before and after (length, width, perimeter, area), comparing sizes, using operations, or creating ratios, fractions, or percentages.

Activity No. 2: Action

With a partner, students choose one transformation to re-create using any tools of their choice (see materials list above). Give them the original blanket size (8'x10') to work from. Encourage them to think realistically for a girl about their size (or about 4'8" tall). Encourage students to discuss their thinking and test their strategies with drawings and computations for reasonableness because they will have to present their work to the class.

Activity No. 3: Presentation

The students will present the information to the class and teacher, with explanations (and possible drawings) of how they created the item and how much material was discarded. The teacher may want to create a rubric for grading. A rubric would include reasoning, multiple solutions, accuracy, cooperation with partner, and defending their thinking.

Middle

Hook

Ask students to reflect on a special childhood belonging, maybe a toy, blanket, T-shirt, or trophy. "How does it make you feel to think about it? Raise your hand if you still have it. Raise your hand if you still use it. In today's lesson a young girl repurposes her special blanket over and over. Let's enjoy the story as we think of the mathematical processes she may have used to create such transformations."

Activity No. 1: Read-Aloud or Independent Reading

The teacher quickly reads the book to students. Be sure students comprehend the Spanish/English words or have the students read the story online before coming to class, noting the words in Spanish.

Activity No. 2: Guided Practice

Have students work with a partner to re-create the blanket into a straight skirt for a given size girl. Use measurements for junior sizes (see resources for chart of dimensions, length is their choice based on what is reasonable). Students collaborate using their process skills and prior mathematical knowledge to re-create the skirt based on the original 8-feet x 10-feet blanket size.

Early finishers should be encouraged to think of what to do with the rest of blanket. The teacher should encourage discussion, observe, question, and take notes on students' thinking as formative assessment and for possible support during independent work.

Activity No. 3: Independent Practice

Assign students to connect to their own lives by designing a plan, including the mathematical thinking needed, to repurpose a towel, blanket, or item of clothing into a useful and meaningful item for their current use or wear. Students must draw out a before and after representation of their item and prepare to explain the process of how they plan to reduce the item's size mathematically and how it is reasonable for the new purpose to a partner.

Activity No. 4: Presentation

The students will present their work to the class and teacher including visuals and explanations of their plan. The teacher may want to assess with the rubric below (see Table 10.1).

Secondary

Hook

Ask students to reflect on a special childhood belonging, maybe a toy, blanket, T-shirt, or trophy. "How does it make you feel to think about it? Raise your hand if you still have it. Raise your hand if you still use it. In today's lesson a young girl repurposes her special blanket over and over. Let's enjoy the story as we think of the mathematical processes she may have used to create such transformations."

Activity No. 1: Independent Reading or Read-Aloud

The teacher quickly reads the book to students. Be sure students comprehend the Spanish/English words or have the students read the story online before coming to class, noting the Spanish words.

Activity No. 2: Guided Practice

Work with a partner to re-create the blanket into a straight skirt for a given size girl. Use measurements for junior (see resources for chart of dimensions, length is their choice based on what is reasonable). Students collaborate using their process skills and prior mathematical knowledge to recreate the skirt based on the original 8-feet x 10-feet blanket size. Students should brainstorm ideas of what to do with the rest of the material from the blanket. The teacher should encourage discussion, observe, question, and take notes on students' thinking as formative assessment and for possible support during independent work.

Activity No. 3: Independent Practice

Assign students to connect to their own lives by designing a plan, including the mathematical thinking needed, to repurpose a towel, blanket, or item of clothing into a useful and meaningful item for their current use or wear. Students will draw out a before and after representation of their item and then create a scaled 3-D model to present with explanation to a partner or small group. Students should be encouraged to demonstrate reasonableness for their new item through mathematics (scale, nets, perimeter/area, geometric thinking, etc.).

Activity No. 4: Presentation

Students will present their work to a partner or small group and include visual representation, a 3-D model, and explanation. The teacher may want to assess with the rubric below (see Table 10.1).

Tips for Struggling/Reluctant Students

Some ways that this lesson can be differentiated to support struggling or reluctant learners include adding more models and/or visuals into the lesson, pairing the student with a more social student, or giving them a more simplified transformation to start with: the skirt to shawl. Include additional student supports such as unitized models (see resources), counting cubes, a number line, or larger-size grid paper for drawing.

Tips for English Language Learners

Some ways that this lesson can be differentiated for English language learners include allowing the student to use the Spanish version, allowing the student to work in their first language, and/or partnering them with someone who is of the same native language but further along in English. Include more visuals with labels in English and their native language.

Evaluation of Skills

- Observation: Take notes of students' mathematical language, their drawings, and explanations.
- Question to check for understanding: "How did you . . . ? Why did you . . . ? What were you thinking . . . ?"
- Take notes while listening to student presentation and discussion: Record possible misconceptions to address, concepts to reinforce, and questions for deeper understanding.
- Evaluate written explanations with drawings for evidence of reasoning and accurate mathematical computations.
- Use a rubric and formally assess the individual project for reasoning skills and computation (see Table 10.1)

Additional Resources

- Different-size grid paper for accuracy with scale: www.waterproofpaper. com/graph-paper/grid-paper.shtml
- Teachers guide for Maya's Blanket (ELAR and more): www.leeandlow. com/books/maya-s-blanket-la-manta-de-maya/teachers_guide
- Elementary Handout (see Figure 10.1)
- Middle Level Handout (see Figure 10.2)

Table 10.1. Rubric for Assessing Individual Project for Reasoning and Computation Skills

Reasoning	Computation	Effort
High: Logical and based on visualization and mathematical understanding of appropriate operations.	High: Accurate 100% of the time	High: Persisting all the way through the lesson, using manipulates/visuals to determine strategies, possibly trying different strategies to solve.
Mid-level: Logical and based on visualization and some math understanding but inappropriate operations.	Mid-level: Accurate most of the time (over 70%).	Mid-level: Making attempts without request for help, utilizing manipulatives and visuals to start.
Low: Based on guessing and poor visualization.	Low: Often inaccurate	Low: Requesting help or shutting down before using manipulatives or visuals to get started.

Directions: Enlarge each image for students to compare sizes.

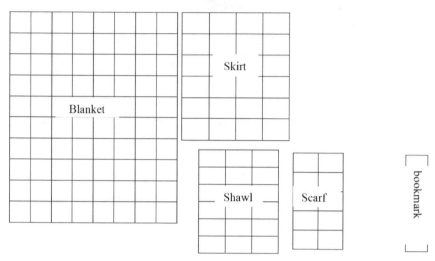

Figure 10.1.   K-2 Comparing Sizes Activity. *Author created.*

CONCLUDING REMARKS

Culturally responsive teaching is often left out of the mathematics classroom as mathematics is thought to be numeral based and often taught in isolation of other contexts. Utilizing stories that feature characters from various cultures solving problems with mathematical reasoning helps students see that mathematics is universal because all people use mathematics to solve problems.

Understanding how mathematics is used universally helps to provide a more global perspective. Using stories like *Maya's Blanket* subtly reinforces this message while affirming the positive traits of the culture. This story subtly reinforces the Hispanic culture by denoting the creativity, intelligence, and loving bonds of the Hispanic characters. The Spanish language is affirmed by

	Waist	Hips	Height
Junior 3-5	27	34	65
Junior 7-9	27.5	36	67
Junior 11-13	28	38	68

Figure 10.2.   Middle Grades Sizing Chart Activity. *Author created.*

the use of the Spanish word (in italics) for each item the blanket changes into and is repeatedly used for the item throughout the text.

REFERENCES

Boaler, J. (2015). *Mathematical mindsets: Unleashing students' potential through creative math, inspiring messages and innovative teaching.* New York: John Wiley & Sons.

Corp, A. (2017). Tea cakes and sweet potato pie for all: Student responses to African American stories in mathematics. *Curriculum and Teaching Dialogue, 19*(1&2), 35–52.

Corp, A. (2018) Purposeful planning: How to be culturally responsive in mathematics. *Texas Mathematics Teacher, 64*(2), 16–21.

Gay, G. (2010). *Culturally responsive teaching: Theory, research, and practice.* New York: Teachers College Press.

Hassinger-Das, B., Jordan, N. C., & Dyson, N. (2015). Reading stories to learn math: Mathematics vocabulary instruction for children with early numeracy difficulties. *The Elementary School Journal, 116*(2), 242–264.

Hefflin, B. R., & Barksdale-Ladd, M. A. (2001). African American children's literature that helps students find themselves: Selection guidelines for grades K–3. *The Reading Teacher, 54*(8), 810–819.

Iliev, N., & D'Angelo, F. (2014). Teaching mathematics through multicultural literature. *Teaching Children Mathematics, 20*(7), 452–457.

Moyer, P. S. (2000). Communicating mathematically: Children's literature as a natural connection. *The Reading Teacher, 54*(3), 246–255.

NCTM (2000). *Principles and standards for school mathematics.* Reston, VA: National Council of the Teachers of Mathematics.

Pérez, C. A. (2012). A story covers all: Using children's literature for acquiring cross-curricular competences in early childhood and primary. *1st International Conference: Teaching Literature in English for Young Learners,* 107–112.

Robertson, K. (2009). Math instruction for English Language Learners: Practical teaching tips for general, bilingual and ESL teachers. *Online Library of Teacher Resource Articles from Colorin, CO, 24.*

Van Garderen, D. (2006). Spatial visualization, visual imagery, and mathematical problem solving of students with varying abilities. *Journal of Learning Disabilities, 39*(6), 496–506.

Van de Walle, J. A., Karp, K. S., Bay-Williams, J. M., Wray, J. A., & Brown, E. T. (2007). *Elementary and middle school mathematics: Teaching developmentally.* London: Pearson.

Conclusion

Barbara Purdum-Cassidy

Historically, the literature presented in public schools represented a "single story," therefore only showing the perspectives and characteristics of white middle-class individualism (Bishop, 1997). However, this "middle-class story" reflects less than half the student population in today's schools (Christ & Sharma, 2018; National Center for Educational Statistics, 2018). *Multicultural Literature in the Content Areas* seeks to remedy the single-story paradigm by providing lessons utilizing multicultural literature to address principles of diversity while addressing curriculum requirements. Culturally diverse texts and affirming pedagogies were featured in each chapter to provide readers with a wide variety of tangible multicultural, multimodal materials and lessons to use in K–12 classrooms.

Culturally diverse texts provide avenues for students to examine and discuss important issues "such as diverse perspectives, intercultural awareness, and breaking down stereotypes and misconceptions. In turn, these types of conversations with children develop general capabilities such as critical and creative thinking, personal and social capabilities, and ethical and intercultural understandings" (Adam & Harper, 2016, p. 1).

However, the selection of culturally diverse texts can be challenging (Adam & Harper, 2016; Christ & Sharma, 2018; Tatum, 2009; Wee, Kura, & Kim, 2018). Research studies document that many authors of children's books are from dominant cultures. These books may include inaccuracies and often perpetuate stereotyping or damaging ideologies (Cai, 1994; Mendoza & Reese, 2001; Yoon, Simpson, & Haag, 2010; Wee, Kura, & Kim, 2018).

Other studies examining the selection of culturally diverse books discuss both the scarcity of culturally diverse children's literature in schools and classrooms as well as selection of instructional texts based on teachers' own cultural and social identities and values (Currie, 2013; Gangi, 2008; Gangi & Ferguson, 2006; Williams 2014). Thus, educators need to become knowledgeable about the selection of culturally diverse books (Christ & Sharma, 2018) and to "use student culture as the basis for helping students understand themselves and others, structure social interactions, and conceptualize knowledge" (Ladson-Billings, 1992, p. 314).

This chapter will provide readers with resources for locating and selecting culturally relevant texts for the classroom. First, a book list that will assist educators in locating culturally relevant texts will be shared. Next, rubrics for assessing the quality of children's books for cultural relevance will be delineated.

LOCATING CULTURALLY RELEVANT TEXTS

Although it can be challenging and time consuming to create a library of culturally relevant books, the benefits to students make this worthwhile. Adam & Harper (2016) point out that teachers should "select books with a variety of genres and cultures and . . . avoid using a single book to represent a particular culture." Table C.1 provides a list of awards that celebrate diversity in children's literature and assists in the selection of culturally relevant texts.

Table C.1.   Award-Winning-Book List for Multicultural Literature

Award and URL	*Criteria for Selection*
American Indian Youth Literature Award http://ailanet.org/activities/ american-indian-youth-literature-award/	Awarded biennially, the AIYLA identifies and honors the best writing and illustrations by and about Native Americans and indigenous peoples of North America.
Arab American Book Award http://arabamericanmuseum.org/ bookaward	Honors books written by and about Arab Americans.
Asian/Pacific American Award for Literature http://apalaweb.org/awards/ literature-awards/	Honors and recognizes individual work about Asian/Pacific Americans and their heritage.
Belpre Medal http://www.ala.org/alsc/ awardsgrants/bookmedia/ belpremedal	Presented annually to the Latino/Latina writer and illustrator who best portrays, affirms, and celebrates Latino culture.
Caldecott Medal http://www.ala.org/alsc/ awardsgrants/bookmedia/ caldecottmedal/caldecottmedal	Awarded annually by the American Library Association to the artist of the most distinguished American picture book for children.

Award and URL	Criteria for Selection
Carter G. Woodson Book Award https://www.socialstudies.org/ awards/woodson	Presented by the National Council for the Social Studies to exemplary books written for children.
Children's Africana Book Award http://africaaccessreview.org/ childrens-Africana-book-awards/ caba-winners/	Presented annually to the authors and illustrators of the best children's and young adult books on Africa published or republished in the United States.
Coretta Scott King Book Award http://www.ala.org/emiert/ cskbookawards	Given annually to outstanding African American authors and illustrators of books for children and young adults that demonstrate an appreciation of African American culture and universal human values.
Dolly Gray Children's Literature Award http://www.dollygrayaward.com/	Given annually by the Division on Autism and Developmental Disabilities (DADD) of the Council for Exceptional Children to recognize effective, enlightened portrayals of individuals with developmental disabilities in children's books.
ILA Notable Books for a Global Society http://clrsig.org/	Selects twenty-five outstanding trade books for enhancing student understanding of people and cultures throughout the world.
Jane Addams Children's Book Award http://www.janeaddamspeace.org/ jacba/	Given annually to a children's book that advances the causes of peace and social equality.
Middle East Book Award http://www.meoc.us/book-awards. html	Recognizes books for children and young adults that contribute meaningfully to understanding the Middle East.
Newbery Medal https://www.ala.org/alsc. awardsgrants/bookmedia/ newberymedal/newberymedal	Awarded annually by the American Library Association to the author of the most distinguished contribution to American literature for children.
Rainbow Book List http://www.ala.org/awardsgrants/ rainbow-project-book-list	Presented to authors whose books highlight LGBTQ content aimed at children and youth from birth to age eighteen.
Schneider Family Book Award http://www.ala.org/awardsgrants/ schneider-family-book-award	Honors an author or illustrator for a book that embodies an artistic expression of the disability experiences for a child and adolescent audience.
Sydney Taylor Manuscript Award http://jewishlibraries.org/content. php?page=Sydney_Taylor_ Manuscript_Award	Awarded for the best fiction manuscript for readers ages eight to thirteen revealing positive aspects of Jewish life.
Tomas Rivera Mexican American Children's Book Award http://www.education.txstate.edu/ ci/riverabookaward/	Honors authors and illustrators who create literature that depicts the Mexican American experience.

CULTURALLY RELEVANT TEXT SELECTION

Once books are located, selecting books that students will find culturally relevant is difficult (Adam & Harper, 2016; Sharma & Christ, 2017; Tatum, 2009). To assist in determining the cultural relevance of a text, rubrics have been developed to assess the extent to which a text may be culturally relevant for a student. Below is a list of rubrics developed to assist with the selection of culturally relevant texts:

- Sharma & Christ (2017) developed the *Cultural Relevance Text Evaluation Rubric*, based on seven dimensions of cultural relevance and knowledge about students: (1) accurate portrayal of culture, (2) author's culture, (3) cultural markers of students, (4) age and gender identity, (5) language or dialect in the story, (6) familiarity of setting of the text, and (7) students' lived experiences.
- Ebe (2010) created the *Cultural Relevance Rubric* to help teachers and students determine the cultural relevance of a text. The rubric asks teachers and students to consider eight aspects of cultural relevance (Goodman, 1982): (1) the ethnicity of the characters, (2) the setting, (3) the year in which the story takes place, (4) the age of the characters, (5) the gender of the characters, (6) the language or dialect used in the story, (7) the genre and exposure to this type of text, and (8) the reader's background experiences.
- Harper & Trostle-Brand (2010) developed the *Checklist for Selecting and Evaluating Multicultural Picture Storybooks* to assess the authenticity of children's books based on the author's authenticity and textual characteristics: (1) accuracy of story, (2) ethnicity of characters, (3) realistic setting, (4) plot depiction and conflicts, (5) theme, (6) accuracy of illustrations, and (7) developmental appropriateness.
- Wilfong (2007) created the *Multicultural Literature Rubric* to assist teachers and students in selecting multicultural young adult literature, based on authority (written by a person from the culture being depicted) and cultural authenticity in terms of characterization, citations or acknowledgments, setting, style, and theme.

CONCLUDING REMARKS

As classrooms become more diverse, the messages that "teachers promote through literature should convey respect and acknowledgement of diversity" (Adam & Harper, 2016, p. 7). Empowering students by providing literature that transports them into worlds they have not experienced (windows) and those in which they can see themselves and their lives mirrored "as part of the larger human experience" sustains students cultures and identities and should be integrated into literacy instruction (Bishop, 1990, p. ix).

It is important to note that not all texts will be culturally relevant for all readers in all the aspects of the rubrics listed above. To match books with readers, it is important for teachers to know themselves, their students, their families, their neighborhoods, and their communities (Kibler & Chapman, 2018).

REFERENCES

Adam, H., & Harper, L. (2016). Assessing and selecting culturally diverse literature for the classroom. *Practical Literacy: The Early & Primary Years, 21*(2), 10–14.

Bishop, R. (1990). Mirrors, windows, and sliding glass doors. *Perspectives, 1*(3), ix–xi.

Bishop, R. (1997). Selecting literature for a multicultural curriculum. In V. J. Harris (Ed.), *Using multiethnic literature in the K–8 classroom* (pp. 1–20). Norwood, MA: Christopher-Gordon.

Cai, M. (1994). Images of Chinese and Chinese Americans mirrored in picture books. *Children's Literature in Education, 25*(3), 169–191.

Christ, T., & Sharma, S. A. (2018). Searching for mirrors: Preservice teachers' journey toward more culturally relevant pedagogy. *Reading Horizons, 57*(1), 55–73.

Currie, A. R. (2013). *Truth be told: African American children's literature in two fourth-grade classrooms.* (Unpublished doctoral dissertation). Oakland University, Rochester, MI.

Ebe, A. E. (2010). Culturally relevant texts and reading assessment for English language learners. *Reading Horizon, 50*(3), 193–210.

Gangi, J. M. (2008). The unbearable whiteness of literacy instruction: Realizing the implications of the proficient reader research. *Multicultural Review, 17*(1), 30–35.

Gangi, J. M., & Ferguson, A. (2006). African American literature: Books to stoke dreams. *Tennessee Reading Teacher, 34*(2), 29–38.

Goodman, Y. M. (1982). Retellings of literature and the comprehension process. *Theory into Practice: Children's Literature, 21*(4), 301–303.

Harper, L. J., & Trostle-Brand, S. (2010). More alike than different: Promoting respect through multicultural books and literacy strategies. *Childhood Education: Journal of the Association for Childhood Education International, 86*(4), 224–233.

Kibler, K., & Chapman, L. A. (2018). Six tips for using culturally relevant texts in diverse classrooms. *The Reading Teacher, 72*(6), 741–744. doi: 10.1002/trtr.1775.

Ladson-Billings, G. (1992). Reading between the lines and beyond the pages: A culturally relevant approach to literacy teaching. *Theory into Practice, 31*(4), 312–320. doi.org/10.108000405849209543558.

Mendoza, J., & Reese, D. (2001). Examining multicultural picture books for the early childhood classroom: Possibilities and pitfalls. *Early Childhood Research and Practice, 32*(2), 35–55.

National Center for Educational Statistics. (2018). *The condition of education.* Retrieved from nces.ed.gov/pubs2018/2018144.pdf

Sharma, S. A., & Christ, T. (2017). Five steps toward successful culturally relevant text selection and integration. *The Reading Teacher, 71*(3), 295–307. doi:10.1002/trtr.1623.

Tatum, A. W. (2009). *Reading for their life: (Re)building the textual lineages of African American adolescent males.* Portsmouth, NH: Heinemann.

Wee, S., Kura, K., & Kim, J. (2018). Unpacking Japanese culture in children's picture books: Culturally authentic representation and historical events/political issues. *Reading Horizons, 57*(2), 35–55.

Wilfong, L. G., (2007). A mirror, a window: Assisting teachers in selecting appropriate multicultural young adult literature. *International Journal of Multicultural Education, 9*(1), 1–13.

Williams, R. (2014). Structure of feeling and selective tradition. In R. Williams (Ed.), *On culture and society* (pp. 27-55). Thousand Oaks, CA: Sage Publishing.

Yoon, B., Simpson, A., & Haag, C. (2010). Assimilation ideology: Critically examining underlying messages in multicultural literature. *Journal of Adolescent & Adult Literacy, 54*(2), 109–118. doi.org/10.1598/JAAL.54.2.3.

About the Editors and Contributors

Lakia M. Scott, PhD, is an assistant professor of urban/multicultural education and literacy at Baylor University. She currently teaches diversity education and literacy methods courses to pre-service teachers and graduate students in the Department of Curriculum and Instruction. Scott has more than a decade of combined experiences at the elementary, secondary, undergraduate, and graduate teaching levels. She is the co-editor of *Culturally Affirming Literacy Practices for Elementary Students* (2016). She has also published several research articles that align with best practices for teaching African American and Hispanic/Latino(a) students. Some of these works include: "White Pre-Service Teachers' Perceptions and their Development of Culturally Relevant Teaching Practices" (2019), "Linguistic Hegemony Today: Recommendations for Eliminating Language Discrimination" (2017), and "English as a Gatekeeper: A Conversation of Linguistic Capital and American Schools" (2014). She is currently conducting research on national reading and language intervention programs, specifically the Children's Defense Fund Freedom Schools Program, which is a literacy program geared toward social action and advocacy issues that directly affect youth while also curbing summer learning loss.

She is the inaugural executive director of the CDF Freedom Schools at Baylor University program. Under her research framework of increasing educational access and opportunities for minoritized youth, she primarily examines urban education programming and initiatives that advance student academic outcomes, multicultural awareness and perspectives in teacher education programs, and Historically Black Colleges and Universities as a gateway for first-generation student success.

Barbara Purdum-Cassidy, EdD, is a clinical associate professor in the Department of Curriculum and Instruction at Baylor University. She currently teaches elementary language arts methods courses to pre-service teachers and graduate students in the Department of Curriculum and Instruction. Cassidy has almost three decades of combined experiences at the elementary, middle, undergraduate, and graduate teaching levels. She is co-editor of *Teaching Literacy in Urban Schools: Lessons from the Field* (2018) and *Culturally Affirming Literacy Practices for Elementary Students* (2016).

She has also published several research articles that examine best practices for teaching urban students. Some of these works include: "Selecting Quality Picture Books for Instruction: What do Preservice Teachers Look For?" (2018), "Beyond Basic Instruction: Effective Civic Literacy Instruction in Urban School Settings" (2016), "An Analysis of the Ways in Which Preservice Teachers Integrate Children's Literature in Mathematics" (2015), and "What Are They Asking? An Analysis of the Questions Planned by Prospective Teachers When Integrating Literature in Mathematics" (2015). Her research interests include creating urban literacy initiatives to advance student academic outcomes, pre-service teachers' enactment of literacy practices, and teacher resilience.

* * *

Amy K. Corp, EdD, is an assistant professor at Texas A&M Commerce. She teaches courses in elementary and mathematics education and supervises student teachers in their field placements. Her research interests are culturally responsive pedagogies in mathematics, integrating mathematics across the curriculum, and mathematical growth mindsets. Dr. Corp can be reached at Amy.Corp@tamuc.edu.

Kelly C. Johnston, EdD, is an assistant professor of literacy education at Baylor University. Dr. Johnston's areas of interest include sociocultural, critical, and affective theories in literacy studies; K–8 literacy pedagogy; and university-school partnerships seeking to improve literacy teaching and learning. Dr. Johnston teaches graduate courses in the Department of Curriculum and Instruction. Before her appointment at Baylor, Dr. Johnston taught graduate courses at Teachers College, Columbia University, and at the City College of New York. Dr. Johnston can be reached at Kelly_Johnston@baylor.edu.

Janet K. Keeler is a journalism instructor and coordinator of the Graduate Food Writing and Photography Certificate Program at University of South Florida St. Petersburg (USFSP). Keeler is a thirty-five-year newspaper veteran and has taught beginning journalism and food writing/photography courses at USFSP since 2011, first as an adjunct, then as a visiting professor, and now as a full-time instructor. A second-year EdD student in education program development at the University of South Florida, Tampa, her research emphasis uses food themes to formulate culturally responsive K–12 and higher education curricula. Janet Keeler can be reached at jkeeler@mail.usf. edu.

Yasmin C. Laird is a newly admitted doctoral student at Baylor University studying educational psychology. Her research interests center on gifted and talented students in foreign language and bilingual education programs. She recently received a master's degree in curriculum and instruction from Baylor University, where, during these studies, she also served as the project director for the Baylor Freedom Schools program. Her experiences in the program inspired her to continue the exploration of multicultural literature as a tool for teaching in the content areas. She can be contacted at Yasmin_Laird@ baylor.edu.

Kevin R. Magill, PhD, is an assistant professor of secondary education at Baylor University specializing in teacher education, critical pedagogy, social studies, literacy, and cultural studies. A former social studies, English language arts, and opportunity teacher, his scholarship examines relationships between ontology, ideology, and pedagogy and how these factors relate to civics teaching and connect to community knowledge. His most recent scholarly works include "The Primacy of Relation: Social Studies Teachers and the Praxis of Critical Pedagogy" and "Critically Civic Teacher Perception, Posture and Pedagogy: Negating Civic Archetypes." Dr. Magill can be reached at Kevin_Magill@baylor.edu.

Christine J. Picot, PhD, is currently a teaching instructor at the University of South Florida in the Department of Childhood Literacy Studies. Her interests include disciplinary literacy, to include academic vocabulary and mathematics problem solving. Her work with pre-service and in-service teachers includes coaching, mentoring, and designing lessons that integrate cross-curricular conceptual learning. Her global work in Mexico highlights the bridge of language and culture to meet the needs of all learners in mathematics problem solving. Dr. Picot can be reached at cmjoseph@mail.usf.edu.

Sarah M. Straub, EdD, is a professor in the College of Education and current Bilingual Education Student Organization (BESO) faculty advisor at Stephen F. Austin State University. Over the course of her ten years in education, Sarah has taught various subjects including Spanish (multiple levels), art, social studies (multiple levels), physical education, and ELAR. Her dynamic experiences in the classroom allow her to develop engaging and meaningful integrative curriculum. In her free time, Sarah enjoys exploring the world and truly delving into the nuances of being a "traveler" versus being a "tourist." Dr. Straub can be reached at straubsm@sfasu.edu.

Elena M. Venegas, PhD, is an assistant professor in the Department of Bilingual and Literacy Studies at the University of Texas Rio Grande Valley. Dr. Venegas has a decade of experience in education across multiple contexts, including as a former elementary school teacher, as a preschool director, and in higher education. Her research interests include social issues in education, Latinx student populations, student-centered approaches to literacy, and reader self-efficacy. Dr. Venegas can be reached at elena.venegas@utrgv. edu.

Jamie Wong graduated from Baylor University with a B.S.Ed. in middle grades mathematics and an M.S.Ed. in curriculum and instruction. She currently teaches seventh-grade mathematics at Lorena Middle School. Her educational interests include access and equity in the classroom and international perspectives in education. Jamie Wong can be reached at jamiejxwong@ gmail.com.